THE CURTAIN RISES

A History of Theater from Its Origins in Greece and Rome
through the English Restoration

Paula Gaj Sitarz

SHOE TREE PRESS
WHITE HALL, VIRGINIA

Published by Shoe Tree Press
an imprint of Betterway Publications, Inc.
P.O. Box 219
Crozet, VA 22932
(804) 823-5661

Cover design by David Wagner
Typography by Typecasting

Library of Congress Cataloging-in-Publication Data

Sitarz, Paula Gaj.
    The curtain rises / Paula Gaj Sitarz.
        p.   cm.
    Includes bibliographical references and index.
    Contents: v. 1. Early origins and Easter theater.
    ISBN 1-55870-198-2 (v. 1): $14.95
    1. Theater — History — Juvenile literature. [1. Theater — History.]
    I. Title.
PN2037.S53   1991
792′.09 — dc20   90-21953
                                                                      CIP

Printed in the United States of America
0 9 8 7 6 5 4 3 2 1

To Michael, Andrew, and Kate with love
and

To Mr. Richard Methia
Who encouraged me to reach for the stars

ACKNOWLEDGMENTS

Special thanks to the many individuals and institutions that were helpful and supportive:

To Adam Broadbent for his inspired illustrations, Joseph Medeiros for his invaluable photographic services, and Laura de Francesco for research assistance.

To the staffs of the New Bedford Free Public Library, New Bedford, Massachusetts; Southworth Library, South Dartmouth, Massachusetts; North Dartmouth Library, North Dartmouth, Massachusetts; and the reference staff at Southeastern Massachusetts University.

And to the following for help in gathering illustrative material:
Dorothy L. Swerdlove, Curator, The Billy Rose Theatre Collection at the Performing Arts Research Center of The New York Public Library; Pamela Jordan, Librarian, Drama Library, Yale University; Kathleen F. Leary, Archivist, Oregon Shakespeare Festival; Caroline Cook, The Asia Society; Joan Schirle, Artistic Director, Dell'Arte; Dennis Powers, Associate Artistic Director, American Conservatory Theatre; Christopher Robinson, Keeper, University of Bristol Theatre Collection; Noelle Guibert, Conservateur, Comédie Française; Nancy Finley, Assistant Curator of Printing & Graphic Arts, The Houghton Library, Harvard University; Jeanne T. Newlin, Curator, Harvard Theatre Collection; Laura S. Wilson, Permissions Assistant, Art Resource; John J. Herrmann Jr., Associate Curator, Department of Classical Art, Museum of Fine Arts, Boston; Lauri S. Lewis, Folger Shakespeare Library; Lisa Brant, Archivist, The Stratford Shakespearean Festival (Ontario); Harvey Sheldon and Mike Hammerson, The Museum of London; Ingrid Thum, Verkehrs- und Reiseburo, Gemeinde Oberammergau; Mrs. E. Tatman, Dulwich Picture Gallery, London; Dr. Klaus–Valtin von Eickstedt, Deutsches Archaeologisches Institut, Athens; Grace Herget, Japan National Tourist Organization; Roberta Cortes, Public Relations Department, National Tourist Office of Spain; Janet Germiller, Office Manager, Michigan Information Transfer Source; Eileen Sullivan, Photograph Library, The Metropolitan Museum of Art; Sherry Byrne, Preservation Librarian, The University of Chicago Library; Dr. Herlinde Menardi, Tiroler Volkskunst–Museum; Victoria & Albert Museum, London; Library of Congress; Bibliotheek der Ryksuniversiteit Utrecht; Herzog Anton Ulrich Museum; Martin Von Wagner Museum; and the National Tourist Organizations of Greece in London and Athens.

And to Barbara Benziger for her encouragement, enthusiasm for this project, and guidance during the early drafts.

CONTENTS

Note to Teachers and Librarians. 9

1. Theatrical Beginnings: The Curtain Rises 11

2. The Golden Greeks: Setting the Foundation 15

3. Roman Theater: From Imitating the Greeks to Bloody Sport . . . 29

4. Medieval Theater: Out of the Church and Into the Street 39

5. The Italian Renaissance: Grand Stages and Dazzling Scenes . . . 53

6. The Italian Renaissance: The Actor's Theater 63

7. The Shakespearean Era: Theater for the People 71

8. Theater in Spain: A Golden Age 89

9. French Neoclassical Theater: From Tears to Laughter 99

10. English Restoration Theater: Privileged Audiences,
    Indecent Comedies. 111

11. Asia: A Different Theater Tradition 121

    Glossary 135
    Suggested Reading 140
    Index 141

NOTE TO TEACHERS AND LIBRARIANS

"Why write a history of the theater from the Greeks to the Restoration with a chapter on Eastern theater traditions for young readers?"

Only a few adults have asked me this question. Most librarians I spoke with were enthusiastic when I mentioned my book. Not only did they view the idea as a novel one, but they saw many applications for it. More on that later. First to the "why."

I became stagestruck at the age of seven when my parents took me to see my first professional theater production. It was a performance of *The Unsinkable Molly Brown.* To me it was magic, and it began my lifelong love of the stage. My parents continued to take me to plays, and in high school I had small roles in school productions.

In my senior year I was lucky enough to take a course in play production taught by Mr. Richard Methia, an inspiring instructor, who later became a finalist in the Teacher in Space program. In his class I began to learn about the history of the theater and how exciting it is.

I decided to pursue this interest and majored in theater history at Smith College, where I studied under Helen Krich Chinoy, a noted theater historian.

Next I went to Simmons College, received my Master of Science degree in library science, and became a children's librarian. On occasion I would receive requests from youngsters ten years old and up for information or a book on the history of the theater, Shakespearean and Greek theater especially. My background and their interests resulted in this project.

At the time, the best I could offer these youngsters was the encyclopedia articles on theater. Unfortunately, I knew these youths wouldn't read in an encyclopedia entry about the many children who have played roles in the theatrical tradition. During the Restoration, when an actress swooned during her death scene, a page boy arranged her gown around her. Boys and girls introduced plays during this period. Boys played the female roles in Shakespearean productions. Children played the parts of angels and shepherds in medieval plays.

My library friends missed the visual images of the theater — actresses holding their faces stiff so their makeup wouldn't crack. These children wouldn't visualize the "Hell Mouth" of the Middle Ages, a huge monster's mouth from which clouds of smoke spewed and actors leaped.

The dramatic story of the theater, the tale of courage and persistence, of obstacles overcome — all are absent in the encyclopedia. Only in a book is there time to detail how companies of boy actors in Shakespeare's time traveled by cart over icy roads to entertain Queen Elizabeth. How else would readers discover that Molière, the great writer of French comedies, toured the countryside with a group of young but poor actors and slept three or more to a bed?

The Curtain Rises is more than a book for stagestruck children, for those who see theater performances or participate in school productions. It's for any youngster or adult who likes an exciting adventure tale. More than anything, *The Curtain Rises* is a story.

What of the other applications that librarians mentioned for this book? One former colleague remarked that when students have an assignment on a cultural aspect of a certain period — Greek, Roman, Medieval, etc. — she can offer my book. A teacher suggested that it can be used as a cultural and sociological history in a curriculum on a country or part of the world. Another teacher pointed out that when students study Greek plays or Shakespeare's plays in English classes, this book will make the study more interesting and help students visualize how the plays were originally performed. A librarian told me that when students ask for a history book to read, she will suggest this book.

I hope this book will be used for any and all these reasons and for others I haven't thought of yet.

1. THEATRICAL BEGINNINGS: THE CURTAIN RISES

Applause. Applause. The curtain rises. The actors and actresses smile and bow to the audience. The scene is a theater — in London's West End, on Broadway, at a local community center, in a cramped schoolroom in South Africa. For plays, players, and playgoers can be found everywhere around the world. But it wasn't always so.

Mystery surrounds the beginnings of the theater. Ancient cave paintings discovered in southwestern France depict men impersonating animals. These primitive men probably acted out the hunt before they went in search of wild game in hopes of having a good hunt. As early as 30,000 years ago, people sang and danced in ceremonies to honor their gods, to call on the gods to save them from earthquakes, plagues, and hunger. The priests and worshippers dressed in animal skins and wore makeup made of ashes or plant juices. But did these people advance from their rituals to theater?

Archaeologists and historians are still trying to fit the pieces of this puzzle together. Paintings on ancient vases and on the walls of pyramids, writings in archaic languages — these are some of the clues that raise more questions than they answer. Do the pictures on the vases represent actors? Are the writings fragments of plays that were acted out? On the walls of a sealed tomb at Abydos in Egypt, a record was found of what might be a religious drama. It is called the *Osiris Passion Play* and it dates to 1887 B.C. The words relate the story of the death and resurrection of the god-king Osiris. Is it the text for a play or for a religious ritual that was repeated in a set way? The debate continues. Maybe you'll get involved in this exciting, ongoing debate and search. For now, we must travel forward to find proof of plays, playwrights, actors, and theaters.

THE GREEKS HONOR THEIR GODS

It's the fifth century B.C. in Athens, Greece. Several times a year, on specific days, the people honor Dionysus, the god of wine and fertility, and give thanks for the grape harvest. Dionysus is one of many gods the Greeks worship. The people at the festival sing, get wildly excited, drink wine, play musical instruments, and dance crazily in a circle on a threshing floor. A chorus of fifty men is dressed as *satyrs*, woodland gods that are half-human, half-animal. Each man wears a shaggy goat's skin, a loincloth with a horse's tail attached, long animal ears, and a snub-nosed mask with a beard. The men dance and chant a hymn or poem called a *dithyramb* in honor of Dionysus. Year after year this ritual occurs until one year plays appear at the sacred festival, too. These early plays are short and simple with much singing and dancing.

Eventually the spring festival, known as the *City Dionysia*, was reorganized into a competition. Ten months before the festival, playwrights who wished to compete submitted their plays to the state officials who presided over the festival. Each playwright wrote four plays: a trilogy of three tragedies, and a *satyr play*. The tragedies were plays about the gods, goddesses, and heroes of Greek legend. The playwrights could draw on much material since Greeks believed in many gods, from Zeus, father of the gods, to Hades, god of the underworld, and Apollo, the god of light. All

A vase painting showing actors portraying horses. Courtesy of Staatliche Museen Zu Berlin.

three tragedies were often written about the same subject. The satyr play was a comedy that poked fun at the tragic theme or story. Since the satyr play developed from the dithyramb, the satyr chorus with their animal costumes was still used. The works of only three playwrights were chosen for the contest.

THE PLAYWRIGHT'S PART

Unlike playwrights today, the playwright of ancient Greece was writer and director; he planned the dances, trained the dancers, wrote the music, and often played the leading role. If he didn't play the leading role, a leading actor was assigned to do so. The state (the government) paid for the actors and for the chorus, who spoke many of the lines. All the other costs were paid by a rich and important citizen called a *choregus*. The state kept a list of the names of wealthy men and assigned them by lot to the playwrights. Imagine being told that you had to pay for the costumes, the props, the training of the chorus, and the musicians. Each playwright hoped for a generous patron and, fortunately, most rich men regarded being a choregus as a civic duty and honor. Many even competed for the privilege. But sometimes the playwright got a man who didn't want to spend much money. One patron, Phokion, an Athenian general and states-

man, was approached by an actor playing the part of a queen. The actor asked if he could have a group of followers on stage dressed in expensive costumes. Phokion refused to pay for the costumes.

THE CITY DIONYSIA

The City Dionysia attracted visitors from all over the Greek world. In Athens it was a week of holiday, for playgoing was not an everyday event. All business was called off and government offices were closed. At first the festival was free, but when the city started charging a fee to attend the performances, poor people were given the money. They were entitled to see the plays, too. Women, who ordinarily were expected to stay at home, and were not permitted to vote or participate in public life, were allowed at the performances. Even prisoners were released from jail to attend.

On the first day of the City Dionysia, the people who would participate in the contests — actors, musicians, chorus members — were introduced; about 1000 people. There was an elaborate procession on the second day of the City Dionysia. Priests and officials carried gifts and animals to sacrifice to the gods. They believed that these sacrifices kept the gods in a good mood. The statue of Dionysus was car-

Theater at Epidaurus showing the circular orchestra. Courtesy of Deutsches Archaeologisches Institut — Athen.

ried through the streets to the outdoor hillside theater where the plays were performed, and then a full day of sports, games, and merry-making followed.

At dawn the next day the members of the audience, dressed in their finest clothes, arrived at the theater with their lunch baskets. Up to 30,000 people sat on backless benches built close together. Some people brought cushions to sit on. From sunrise until sundown they watched plays, as many as five plays in one day. They saw tragedies, satyr plays, dithyrambs, and in later years comedies as well. Could you sit and watch that long with only one intermission? The audience was expected to be on their best behavior, too,

although they hissed and booed actors they didn't like or pelted them with dried fruit. Staff bearers maintained order and reprimanded offenders. On the final day of the festival, punishments were handed out with violent actions punishable by death.

The final day of the festival was also devoted to criticizing the plays and awarding prizes. The winning playwright was brought to the stage and crowned with a wreath of ivy. Later he held a grand banquet for friends, actors, and members of the chorus. These playwrights were highly honored by the people and encouraged by the city-state. Some playwrights held public office.

THESPIS: THE FATHER OF PLAYWRIGHTING

Imagine how exciting it must have been for the playwright who won that first competition. The playwright's name was Thespis. More important than being the first winner, he is remembered for being the first person who dared to step away from the chorus of fifty men, to answer the chorus, to speak lines by himself — not narrating events but assuming the *character* of someone else — and so became the first actor. This was a brave act because only kings and priests were allowed to speak apart from the chorus.

We still honor Thespis with the English word *thespian*, which means "dramatic" or "actor." At the time, however, many people were shocked. One Athenian lawmaker named Solon told Thespis how outrageous and dangerous he thought his behavior was. He asked Thespis how he could lie in front of so many people. Solon thought acting — pretending to be someone else — was lying.

Thespis opened the door to many wonderful possibilities. There could be dialogue, talk between the actor and the chorus. Thespis started new trends in Greek theater that would not end there.

2. THE GOLDEN GREEKS: SETTING THE FOUNDATION

The daring Thespis was followed by the poet-playwright Aeschylus, who added a second actor, and Sophocles, who added a third. Drama was no longer mainly a series of long poems performed by the chorus. Now, acting, dialogue, and character development would become as important as the lyrical passages. A time traveler from our century to Athens, Greece in the fifth century B.C. might report on such a theatrical performance in this way:

A TIME TRAVELER'S REPORT

"Even though I had arrived at 4 a.m. at the Theater of Dionysus, I had to sit on a wooden bench far up the hillside. But I was more fortunate than those who later sat high among the rubble and stones. Oh, they could see fine, everyone had a good view. But they were a bit uncomfortable. When the sun rose, the first play was announced. I saw the high priest sitting in the middle front row with other high officials to either side of him. I overheard the man next to me exclaim, 'Ah, so the poet Sophocles is presenting this myth. I wonder how he'll treat this sad tale.'

"Twelve men wearing masks marched from an opening on the right onto a flat circular area in a hollow far below me. Their masks were painted with dark curly hair, down-turned mouths, and eyes outlined in thick black. The men wore colorful, decorated, long-sleeved tunics that covered them from neck to ankle.

"This group of men related the events in the story before the moment when the play began. Then the three actors appeared, masked and robed. Their movements were slow, graceful, and dignified. As the actors spoke and sang to each other, the story unfolded. Sometimes the chorus leader spoke to the actors. Often the chorus chanted to the other characters. As high up as I was, I could hear every line of verse.

"I saw no scenery, no painted trees or furnished rooms. Oh, there were a few props — a torch, a sword, a tent. Behind the flat playing area was a small wooden building. The actors went in and out of it often to change their masks and reappear as different characters.

"Toward the end of the play a messenger spoke of horrible deeds, murder and violence, but we didn't see these actions on stage. Later, actors representing dead bodies were wheeled out on a platform. Finally, when it seemed that nothing would be resolved, an actor wearing the mask of a god was lowered in a chariot from the top of the building in back. He untangled the characters' problems. When the play ended I felt awed, satisfied, and uplifted."

THE GREEK THEATER SPACE

Our time traveler was surprised at how different the classical Greek theater was from his own. He could only view plays during the day because Greek theaters were open-air spaces. There were no indoor or lighted theaters, no curtains or roofs. The audience was at the mercy of the weather. If it rained, they got wet.

The Greek theater had begun as a round playing area with an altar surrounded by bleachers and a temple nearby. The temple was built to honor a specific god, to keep him or her happy, to provide the god with a home. Over time the theater's form developed and

Theater of Dionysus in Athens. Courtesy of National Tourist Organization of Greece, Athens.

Modern theater production in the theater at Epidaurus. Courtesy of National Tourist Organization of Greece, Athens.

changed, but the classical Greek theater remained simple. The audience sat in the *theatron*, which means "seeing place," and from which we get the word *theater*. The theatron was tiers of seats surrounding the playing space in a horseshoe all the way up the hillside. The theatron had wedge-shaped divisions separated by aisles. The Greeks often located their theaters in a natural hollow between two hillsides. From above, the theater looked bowl-shaped.

The flat circular area where the chorus and the actors performed was called the *orchestra*. In the middle of the orchestra there was an altar. The building behind the playing area, the *skene* (from which we get the word "scene"), was at first a temporary wooden structure with a flat roof. It was not always behind the orchestra. Before the classical period it had been further away, but it wasn't convenient for the actors to run to the skene to change their masks. While the skene served as a background for the action, it was first built as a storage room for masks, equipment, and props and as a dressing room for the actors. Later dressing rooms for the actors and the chorus were attached to the sides of the skene. Called *paraskenia*, these were rectangular rooms projecting in front of the skene on both sides.

Masks of Greek actors. Courtesy of The Billy Rose Theatre Collection, The New York Public Library at Lincoln Center, Astor, Lenox, and Tilden Foundations.

Between the theatron and the skene were two side entrances called *paradoi* through which the chorus could reach the orchestra. The audience entered here as well, crossed the orchestra, and climbed to their seats up the hillside. None of these parts of the theater was connected to any other.

As our time traveler discovered, the acoustics of the theater were fantastic. If you visit the remains of the theater at Epidaurus in Greece and someone strikes a match in the orchestra, you can hear it in the farthest seats of the theater. The ruins of this theater are used for an annual festival where ancient Greek plays are performed in modern Greek language.

MASKS AND COSTUMES

The actors' masks that so impressed our time traveler were made of cork, linen, or carved and painted wood. A mask larger than the actor's face fit like a helmet over his head. The masks had exaggerated features so viewers high on the hillside could see them clearly.

There were specific masks for different characters, and they were used in play after play. Each mask showed the main personality trait of the character — hate, fear, or stupidity, for example. One mask had bushy white hair with a full beard and jutting eyebrows. The painted mask worn by the actor playing Oedipus in the play *Oedipus Rex* was bloodstained and blinded. At a glance the audience knew the age, mood, and social status of the character. This was useful since there were no theater programs.

Masks also identified the sex of the character. Since women were not allowed to act in the classical Greek theater, all the parts were played by men. The masks for female characters were light-colored, while those for male characters were dark. Masks allowed each of the three actors to play several roles, so a play could have many characters.

Our time traveler remarked on the movements and costumes of the actors. In addition to the brilliantly colored, long-sleeved, full-length robes, the tragic actors wore soft leather boots with low soles. The costume was a total disguise meant to mask the actor's features and personality. It was believed that a complete covering was necessary so the tragic actor could give up his identity to represent gods and heroes.

If the time traveler had watched a comedy during the classical age, the actors would have moved in a more lively and exaggerated manner. Their tunics would have been shorter, often too tight, and heavily padded in the bellies and backsides.

THE ACTORS AND THE CHORUS

In tragedies and comedies the actor's most important asset was his voice. Since his face was hidden behind a mask, the actor had to express emotion through his voice. He also had to change his voice to suit the various characters he played. The actor's voice had to carry over great distances, too, and he trained like an opera singer. Some actors specialized in weird sounds—waves, the wind, and animal cries.

The chorus was an oddity to our time traveler. At one time with as many as fifty members, the chorus represented a range of characters including old men, maidens, birds, fish, frogs, goats, and clouds. They often wore hideous animal masks in comedies. The chorus members wore disguises appropriate to the characters they portrayed. In Aeschylus' play *The Furies*, the chorus dressed in black and wore masks with writhing snake heads. Sometimes they simply wore accessories to suggest their characters, like feathered wings. In *The Clouds* by Aristophanes the chorus wore women's masks with big noses. The chorus' training was extensive. Not only did they memorize their lines, but they also learned music and dance steps. Singing or chanting their lines in unison, the chorus was used to give advice, express an opinion, ask the characters questions, set the mood, react to the events on stage, or comment on action to come. The chorus was a strong presence and could express a deep emotion sometimes merely by

Artist's interpretation of a Greek tragic mask. Illustration by Adam Broadbent.

standing still. As the actors became more important, the role of the chorus gradually lessened; their numbers were reduced until the chorus was no longer used.

STAGING THE PLAYS

The actor seen by the time traveler being lowered to the stage from the roof of the skene rode in a crane or *mechane*. Usually a god, perhaps Athena or Heracles, appeared in the crane. The god often arrived at the end of the play to resolve all the conflicts and tangles in the characters' lives. This god was called the *deus ex machina*, which means "the god from the machine." Sometimes the crane showed characters fleeing or suspended above earth. Scenes of violence were taboo in the Greek theater, so murders happened offstage. However, a platform or couch on wheels called the *ekkyklema* was rolled out through the central

A Greek actor holding a tragic mask and wearing high boots. Courtesy of Martin Von Wagner Museum der Universität Würzburg.

A modern theatrical production showing the chorus, in the theater of Epidaurus. Courtesy of National Tourist Organization of Greece, London.

A modern theatrical production in the theater at Epidaurus. Courtesy of National Tourist Organization of Greece, Athens.

door of the skene carrying the bodies of characters killed offstage to show the aftermath of horrible deeds. The ekkyklema also could be used to show indoor scenes.

Aeschylus introduced as a scenic element the painted canvases in wooden frames called *pinakes*. They could be placed in front of the skene to suggest the location of the play. Paintings on ancient vases tell us that on occasion set pieces made of wood were used. The most popular set piece seems to be the entrance to a cave framed by rocks.

Scenery was not used very much. Instead, the playwright's words painted vivid pictures. The play, written in verse, was the most important aspect of the classical Greek theater. The words were so moving in Greek tragedies that the audience felt as if they had gone through the experiences of the characters. Aristotle, a Greek critic and philosopher, later explained in his book *The Poetics* that Greek tragedies aroused people's emotions of pity and fear and then purged or cleansed people of these feelings, leaving them feeling stronger, enriched.

GREEK TRAGEDY

Aristotle's explanation of Greek tragedy was read by later generations and used as a guide for what tragedy should be. So tragedy has come to us through the generations in a direct line from the Greeks. Greek tragedies are concerned with man's fate in a world where the gods are involved in men's actions and lives. Greeks believed that the gods and the goddesses lived on Mount Olympus and watched the Greek people and made sure they behaved.

The hero of these tragedies is a good man who regards himself as equal to or superior to the gods. The tragic hero often faces a difficult moral choice. He chooses a course of action often knowing that he will have to suffer because of it. An error, perhaps a flaw in his character or ignorance about something, trips him up. He struggles against powers he can't control or understand. The theme is man versus a fate he cannot escape because it is predestined.

The Playwrights

The most noted writers of Greek tragedy were Aeschylus, Sophocles, and Euripides. Between them they wrote more than 150 plays. They based their plays on existing myths and ancient Greek legends and wrote about heroes and gods who were familiar to the audience. But, although the audience knew the story and its outcome, they still were held in suspense. They were interested in seeing how the playwright treated a particular story, through his insight, his poetry, and the performance. These plays were so well written that several are still performed and used as models for contemporary plays. The modern play *Equus* has the same structure as *Oedipus Rex* by Sophocles.

The oldest plays in existence were written by Aeschylus, who is known as "the father of Greek tragedy" and is considered the real founder of European drama. For forty years Aeschylus participated in the dramatic contests. Only one performance of any given play was given at the City Dionysia in Athens, so it is a testimony to Aeschylus' genius that after his death his plays were revived by special decree. His ninety plays, seven of which have survived to our time, are mainly about men who come in conflict with the laws of the gods. Men purposely violate these laws and then are punished for their crimes by what is called "divine justice." Often the punishment is carried on to many generations of the same family. In his grand trilogy *The Oresteia* and in other plays, Aeschylus sought to make sense out of the world and man's place in it. Legend has it that Aeschylus died when an eagle dropped a tortoise on his head.

Sophocles also was concerned with man's inability to escape his fate and the relationship between men and the gods. But, while Aeschylus wrote of abstract problems, Sophocles

Douglas Campbell as Oedipus, courtesy of the Stratford (Ontario) Shakespeare Festival, Canada.

ΑΛΚΗΣΤΙΣ
ΑΡΧΕΛΑΟΣ
ΑΙΓΕΥΣ
ΑΙΟΛΟΣ
ΑΛΟΠΗ
ΑΝΤΙΓΟΝΗ
ΑΝΗΛΙΩΝ
ΑΝΔΡΟΜΕΔΑ
ΑΛΕΞΑΝΔΡΟΣ
ΑΥΓΗ
ΑΝΔΡΟΜΑΧΗ
ΑΝΤΙΓΟΝΗ
ΑΥΤΟΛΥΚΟΣ
ΒΑΚΧΑΙ
ΒΓΛΛΕΡΟΦΟΝΤΗΣ
ΒΟΥΣΕΙΡΙΣ
ΔΙΚΤΥΣ
ΔΑΝΑΗ
ΕΙΦΙΓΕΝΕΙΑ
ΕΛΕΝΗ
ΕΙΝΩ
ΕΚΑΒΗ
ΕΡΡΙΧΘΕΥΣ
ΕΥΡΥΣΘΕΥΣ
ΕΠΕΟΣ

ΚΡΗΤΕΣ
ΚΡΗΣΣΑ
ΚΡΕΣΦΟΝΤΥΣΣ
ΚΥΚΛΩΨ
ΛΙΚΥΜΝΙΟΣ
ΜΕΛΛΝΙΠΠΟΣ
ΜΗΔΕΙΑ
ΜΕΛΕΑΓΡΟΣ
ΟΙΝΕΥΣ
ΟΙΔΙΠΟΥΣ
ΟΡΕΣΤΗΣ

A statue of Euripides. Courtesy of The Billy Rose Theatre Collection, The New York Public Library at Lincoln Center, Astor, Lenox, and Tilden Foundations.

wrote about specific dilemmas and individual characters. He wrote about men bravely dealing with terrible crises in their lives, individual men who struggle against fate. In *Oedipus Rex*, considered the greatest Greek tragedy, Oedipus, King of Thebes, discovers that he has killed his father and married his mother. Oedipus blinds himself and goes into exile. *Oedipus Rex* is one of the most often produced plays of our times.

Euripides was ahead of his time with his political insight and attempts to take traditional myths and change them for his own purposes. He questioned traditional values and Greek society, poked fun at the gods, and explored abnormal psychology in his plays. In *Medea* the main character murders her children. Euripides explored the conflicts within man rather than man at odds with the gods. His heroes were ordinary men with all their flaws and faults showing. Sophocles and Aeschylus showed almost superhuman heroes.

Athenians were uneasy about this poet Euripides, who publicly condemned war in his play *The Trojan Women* at a time when the Greeks were at war. He also depicted the gods as petty, much less than perfect. Euripides was ridiculed by other dramatists and eventually banished from Athens. His works became more popular after his death, and now Euripides is regarded as the first feminist because he created some of the best female characters found in plays.

GREEK COMEDY

Comedy entered the festivals fifty years after tragedy. Comedies interest and amuse people. They make us laugh, and the action usually resolves happily for the main characters. Aristophanes was the main poet of Old Comedy. In his plays, he abused and satirized by name politicians, philosophers, other playwrights, anyone he didn't like or who seemed to be working against the best interests of the people. The actors in Aristophanes' plays wore masks that were caricatures of the people they represented. In one play, *The Clouds*, Aristophanes made fun of the philosopher Socrates. Socrates was in the audience and he stood up so the people could see the resemblance between him and the mask of the actor who played him. Sometimes Aristophanes reprimanded the people of Athens, too. He wanted to point out their faults and foolishness. The *idea* he was conveying in the play, not the plot, was Aristophanes' main focus. Sometimes he interrupted the play to speak directly to the audience on topics unrelated to the story. Although he tackled controversial topics and used indecent language, Aristophanes was rarely censored during this time of democracy in Athens, a time of freedom of speech when all men except slaves and foreigners could vote and speak at weekly meetings about how the city should be run.

One hundred years after Aristophanes, Menander wrote what is called New Comedy, and he set the standard for comedy for centuries. As recently as 1957 one of his plays, *The Curmudgeon,* was discovered in Cairo, Egypt. The subject of Menander's more than 100 plays was man's private, everyday life — family relationships, money, and love problems. He observed the rich middle class in Athens and wrote about them. In these plays fate doesn't control actions against man but chance, accidents, and coincidences do. Menander invented "stock figures," character types who appear in play after play, like the

Artist's interpretation of the masks of comedy and tragedy. Illustration by Adam Broadbent.

miserly old man and the scheming slave. Another popular type was the old nurse, whose mask is that of a homely old woman with a snub nose and two teeth. Another is the parasite, who lives off of his fortunate friends, and his mask sports a high, bald, smooth forehead with a hooked nose. In many comedies eating and drinking were important. This meant lots of food cooked by kitchen slaves whose masks had bald heads and round red faces.

AFTER THE CLASSICAL AGE

While beautiful verse was the premier element of theater in classical Greece, the performer and special effects were the focus of the Hellenistic theater that followed. There we find raised stages, seven foot high actors, and revolving prisms.

The golden age of Athens, Greece during the fifth century B.C. was an important time, a time when most people could participate in government and did, and the government supported the arts. The conditions were perfect for outstanding creative works in architecture, poetry, literature, philosophy, and medicine. In this short period of about 150 years, a large and enduring collection of fine drama developed and matured and would live to reach us 2000 years later.

Greek actors. Courtesy of National Tourist Organization of Greece, Athens.

Theater in Greece changed in several important ways during the Hellenistic Age, which began after the death of Alexander the Great. Athens was no longer an independent democracy but a colony of Macedonia. People paid more attention to their personal lives than to public affairs.

DESIGN OF THE THEATER

If you could travel back in time and visit a Greek theater during the Hellenistic period, you would see a raised stage between the skene and the orchestra. The stage was supported by huge pillars, and it stood 10 to 12 feet above the orchestra. The stage wasn't very deep but it was long—more than half the length of a football field.

The orchestra was much smaller than before and was often a semi-circle rather than a circle. The skene was no longer a temporary wooden house. Now it was an impressive stone structure with massive columns. The skene had one to three doors, which allowed actors to enter the stage from the back.

Periaktoi were used on the Hellenistic stage. These were tall, triangular prisms set at either side of the skene. Scenes were painted or hung on each side and the periaktoi revolved to suggest a change of location. For example, one side could show waves to represent the sea. Turn the periaktoi and you'd see ships to represent a harbor. A third turn would reveal trees to depict a forest.

ACTORS LARGER THAN LIFE

If you sat on one of the new permanent stone seats in the auditorium, you would see actors who looked larger than life. The tragic actor wore thick-soled, high boots and a tall headdress, which included a mask and an attached wig. If the actor removed the boots and the headdress, you would see a 7-foot, 6-inch actor become a 6-foot tall person. These innovations in costuming were necessary so the actor wouldn't look like an ant on the large stage.

New Comedy was more popular than tragedy during this period. Comic actors in these plays omitted the padding used in Old Comedy. Instead, they wore costumes based on the dress of ordinary life.

Masks, including the mouthpiece, were enlarged and exaggerated. The wide, upturned mouth on the mask for comedy and the wide, downturned mouth on the mask for tragedy became the symbols for the theater worldwide.

ACTORS AS STARS

Acting was supreme during this period, much more important than playwriting. The Hellenistic age had stars like our movie and television personalities. Some actors changed the play scripts to show off their talents or removed their masks to reveal their individual personalities.

Famed actors were so highly regarded that sometimes they were exempt from military service. Often they were safe from arrest if they committed a crime. Actors could travel and perform in states that were at war with each other, for their safety was guaranteed. Sometimes actors served as ambassadors to bring peace between warring states.

Actors even formed professional organizations called *guilds*. In a guild you could find playwrights, actors, chorus members, musicians, and costumers—everyone you needed to put on a play. Choregoi no longer funded plays. Instead, elected officials were given money from the state. Each official paid a guild to put on a performance at a festival. They presented the plays of classical Greece, often in the homes of rulers. By performing these plays in their own and other countries, the guild members helped preserve and introduce classical drama to a larger part of the world.

As time passed, few new plays were written. The Greek theater declined as the Romans started gaining power. Greece had witnessed a long and glorious period of drama and acting known as "The Golden Age."

3. ROMAN THEATER: FROM IMITATING THE GREEKS TO BLOODY SPORT

Rome, Italy was uncivilized during Athens' golden age. While Athenians enjoyed the plays of Aeschylus and Sophocles, Romans watched primitive plays and improvised comic scenes performed by wandering troupes of players on makeshift stages. But Rome conquered Greece during the Roman Republic (509-27 B.C.), a period when Rome was ruled by a representative body including a Senate and citizen assemblies. Naturally, the Romans were influenced by Greek culture, and Roman playwrights imitated the Greek comedies and tragedies for their stages.

THE ROMAN FESTIVALS

In 240 B.C. Livius Andronicus was the first playwright to adapt Greek comedies and tragedies and translate them into Latin. Andronicus' plays were produced at the *Ludi Romani*, a religious festival in honor of the god Jupiter. The ancient Romans, like the Greeks, believed in hundreds of gods. Each family worshipped a special household god. Also like the Greeks, the Romans wanted to keep the gods happy with sacrifices and presents. Plays now were performed alongside the other entertainment, which included athletic events, gladiator fights, rope-dancing, boxing, acrobats, beast fights, circus races, music, and dances. These amusements were considered pleasing to the many gods they were meant to honor.

Eventually there were five annual public festivals associated with the state religion and given in honor of various gods. At first the plays were offered with the other entertainment and games in the Circus Maximus, a large arena for chariot races, which could hold many people. Politicians or other wealthy men paid for the festivals, and magistrates supervised them. The men who sponsored the festivals spent more and more money to win the public's favor. They thought they might advance their political careers if the people thought they had provided them with great entertainment. And many important citizens attended the festivals, people who could vote for or against the man who sponsored a festival.

Since the dramatic performances were provided free by state authorities, they did not allow comments or dialogue in plays that said anything negative about officials or the way they managed the government. Aristophanes would not have seen his plays produced in Republican Rome.

THE ROMAN THEATERS

At first there were no permanent theaters in Rome. Stages were erected in the large circuses, or simple temporary wooden buildings were put up. Each building had a wooden stage, an orchestra, and tiers of seats. A dressing room was directly behind the stage, and its front wall was the back-scene of the stage. Over time these temporary theaters became bigger and more elaborate.

These Roman theaters were erected for the feast days of gods and for other specific occasions when games were held including public holidays, funerals to honor dead noblemen, the birthday of an emperor, and the celebration of military victories. The theaters were built in public places near temples. Even when these temporary buildings were ornately decorated, they were torn down after the festival

Setting for Andria *by Terence from a 1493 Lyons edition of the play. Courtesy of Drama Library, Yale University.*

because state officials were opposed to permanent theater buildings. The officials considered permanent buildings unnecessary since the large circuses already existed for most games and entertainments.

ROMAN COMEDIES AND TRAGEDIES

In the Roman theaters, the people saw comedies and tragedies based on Greek plays. Roman writers either used Greek subject matter and characters or modified the Greek plays to relate Roman stories and ideas. Often they translated the Greek plays with few changes. Only fragments of tragedies written during the Republic of Rome have survived. We do have several comedies written by Plautus (Titus Maccius Plautus) and Terence (Publius Terentius Afer). Plautus adapted the Greek New Comedy of Menander and others and made it appealing to Roman audiences. He didn't just translate the Greek plays; he placed the action in Rome and used everyday details of Roman life. Plautus' plots are lively and fast-paced. There are misunderstandings based on mistaken identity and sometimes sons who spend a lot of money and fool their fathers. One of Plautus' favorite themes was a young man in love with the daughter of an important person and the way in which a slave helps the young man win the girl through trickery. Plautus' plays are full of jokes and music and wildly funny characters including the old man in love with his money, the young man who rebels against his parents, the scheming slave, the bragging yet cowardly soldier, and the unpleasant wife.

Terence was brought to Rome as a slave from Africa while still a young boy and later freed. While he, too, based his plays on Greek New Comedy, Terence did not write the wild and nutty plays with exaggerated characters and offensive language that Plautus did. Terence often wrote about the romance between young people. He also liked to contrast characters like two brothers, one timid and one bold. Terence's interest was in people, and he tried to write carefully about characters rather than concentrating on the story line.

Through Plautus' and Terence's plays, Greek New Comedy survived. Because they used so many elements from Greek comedies, we know a lot about the Greek plays and playwrights. Plautus' and Terence's plays left their mark on the theater in other ways. Terence's plays influenced writers in the Middle Ages and the Renaissance. Playwrights through time have borrowed Plautus' plots and characters. In England William Shakespeare based *The Comedy of Errors* on two of Plautus' plays. The successful 1962 American musical *A Funny Thing Happened on the Way to the Forum* was also based on a combination of Plautus' plays. Many Roman comedies were interrupted by songs, just as American musical comedies are.

STAGING THE ROMAN PLAYS

Plautus and Terence saw their plays first staged in the temporary wooden theaters. It wasn't until 55 B.C. that Pompey was allowed to build the first permanent stone theater in Rome. Before this time Roman designers probably built and tore down more than 500 theaters. Ultimately there were three permanent theaters in Rome. The Romans had learned to build arches, and this allowed them to create massive theaters. Roman theaters differed from Greek theaters in other ways, too. The Roman theater was built on flat ground, and in the Roman theaters the scene house, the stage, the orchestra, and the auditorium were joined by a wall which was the same height all around.

The stage of the Roman theater was low, about five feet high. It was from 100 to 300 feet long, from half a football field to the length of an entire football field. The actors performed on a stage that was 20 to 40 feet deep, and they didn't worry about rain because the stage had a roof. Even the audience was protected from rain and burning sun by linen awnings.

The orchestra shrank to a semi-circle. The performers didn't act here, but the orchestra was used to seat important people including senators and visiting dignitaries. Sometimes the orchestra was used for dancing and animal fights, and it was even flooded for water ballets.

The most outstanding feature of the theater was the *scaenae frons*, an elaborate stage wall which you will remember as the skene. Here it was two to three stories high, decorated with columns and statues. Niches and alcoves were cut into the backstage, and special decorations including hanging wreaths and bronze ornaments were placed here. The Roman philosopher and writer Cicero claimed that the scaenae frons was painted or covered in gold in some theaters.

The scaenae frons was used as a background for the action. In comedy it represented a series of houses with the stage as a city street. In tragedy it was the front of a palace or a temple. Of course, that limited the locations where a play could be set. Since there was no way to represent indoor scenes all the action had to take place in open-air places.

The scaenae frons had three doors which were used as entrances for the actors and as part of the action. For example, a character could pretend to hear conversations behind the doors, or a squeaking door could be used to warn of someone approaching. The Romans used a curtain on their stage. It was used to hide the stage before the play began. Instead of raising the curtain the Romans lowered it with telescoped poles into a wide trench at the front of the stage.

Roman theater at Orange, France. Courtesy of Giraudon/Art Resource.

THE THEATERGOERS AND WHAT THEY SAW

Crowds of spectators, sometimes 40,000 people, streamed into these theaters through a series of vaulted entrances, staircases, and passageways leading to doors in each section of each level of the auditorium. These doors were called *vomitoria* because they spit out (vomit) the thousands of theatergoers. By having these separate entrances people didn't crush each other in their rush to get a seat.

Whether attending the grand stone theaters or the temporary ones, everyone went to the theater for free, all classes of men, women, and sometimes children. The different classes of people were seated in different areas, separated by barriers. The crowds laughed, quarreled, and shouted at each other. They commented on the officials in the front seats, booed or cheered the man who sponsored the games. Often they left the theater to watch some other entertainment like rope-dancing or boxing. Spectators went outside the theater to buy drinks, fruits, or other treats from a vendor. Sometimes the audience was cooled by an enormous spray of perfumed water. These festivals were major social occasions. Ancient Romans loved to be entertained, and they knew how to have a good time.

Special effects and individual performances were more important than playwrights in Rome. Dramatists didn't have the close connection with the theater that the Greeks did. Roman playwrights sold their plays to producers who mounted the productions.

The Actors

Actors adopted the Greek style of acting and staging a play. In comedies they wore a short tunic and cloak with flat sandals or soft slippers. Wigs of different colored hair attached to the masks and revealed their character. A white wig indicated an old man, a red wig represented a slave, and a young man wore a black wig. In tragedies the actors' high boots were even higher than in the Hellenistic age, with wooden blocks for heels. Actors wore padding so they wouldn't look like thin pretzels on stilts. The mask had a high peak of painted hair over the forehead and elaborate, full, twisted locks of hair down the sides. Masks were exaggerated, like those of the Hellenistic age, with wide mouth openings. The Roman performances differed in one important way from the Greek: there was no longer a limit on the number of performers used in a play.

Performers usually specialized in the type of roles they played. The comic actor Demetrius played gods, good fathers, young men, and respectable old men. Stratocles preferred to play cunning slaves and mean-tempered old men. From the first century B.C., instead of presenting an entire play, actors selected scenes to display their special talents. If the audience clapped loudly after an actor spoke, the actor would repeat what he had just said.

The greatest and most popular Roman actor was the comic Quintus Roscius Gallus, known as Roscius. He specialized in playing women, gods, and young people. During the 19th century, performers wanted to be called a "Roscius" because it was a label for a fine actor. In his own time Roscius was given a gold ring and the rank of knight by the Emperor Sulla.

In spite of Roscius' fame and the fact that spectators had their favorite performers, whom they cheered and rioted over, actors were held in low regard. Actors in Rome did not enjoy the high social status Greek actors had. Roman actors could not vote or hold political office. Most were from the lower classes and were treated like slaves. During the later years of the Roman Empire, many acting troupes were made up entirely of foreign slaves. The managers of troupes trained and paid the actors, but they were mainly interested in making money. These managers were strict disciplinarians and treated the actors as they wished. If the audience booed an

Roman actors. Courtesy of the University of Michigan.

Statuette of Roman comic actor. Courtesy of Museum of Fine Arts, Boston, H. L. Pierce Fund.

Roman comic father mask. Courtesy of the University Museum, University of Pennsylvania.

actor, the manager whipped him.

The art of acting deteriorated more and more during the Empire (27 B.C.–476 A.D.), when Rome was ruled by emperors rather than a representative group, and emperors were worshipped as gods after they died. The Roman Emperor Nero was an evil ruler who ruthlessly killed people, but that didn't shock the people as much as his appearances on the stage. That shows the low regard in which actors were held.

During these hard times, the people preferred to forget their troubles and to watch *mime* and *pantomime* more than comedies and tragedies. Women appeared on stage in the mime. This was a first. Unlike mimes of today who don't speak, the small troupes that performed the Roman mimes did speak. They also performed without masks, unlike the actors in Greek and Roman comedies and tragedies. Each person played a character type: an old man, a young woman, or perhaps a scheming slave. Some characters had a special talent for mimicry, neighing like a horse, for example.

The Story Line

The performers used a simple story line that was familiar and then filled out the plot by making up or improvising the dialogue. The play was usually about something funny from everyday life, just like a situation comedy on television. The mimes were short and often ended suddenly. Sometimes an animal, a dog, for example, had the main role, like Benji in the movies. Mime troupes also provided entertainment including tightrope walking and sword swallowing. Eucharis was a female mime who already had a great reputation as a performer when she died at age fourteen.

Known as "storytelling dance," pantomime usually starred one masked dancer who silently told a story through movement and gesture. He played all the roles by changing masks. A chorus sang the story line, which took themes from mythology or history and often centered on the theme of love. Pantomimes included music, flutes, pipes, cymbals, and fantastic special effects. One pantomime produced during this era had a setting that included a fake mountain of wood. It was planted with shrubs and living trees and featured a running stream and goats at the top. For the ending the mountain spouted wine colored with saffron, which sprinkled over the white goats and dyed them yellow. A gaping hole then opened and swallowed the mountain of wood.

During the Roman Empire, people became more and more interested in *spectacles*. The emperors who now ruled were tyrants who terrorized people. The people no longer enjoyed many freedoms or participated in civic affairs. They were interested in comfort and thrills, in forgetting their troubles. Playwrights and actors had to compete even more with the other entertainment offered in the circuses and amphitheaters nearby. Playwrights knew their serious plays wouldn't be watched because people wanted to be amused, and emperors wouldn't let the writers speak the truth about Roman life in their plays. Some authors reacted by writing plays to be read only, not performed.

The Tragedies of Seneca

The only Roman tragedies that have survived to our time were written during the Empire by Lucius Annaeus Seneca. Seneca's plays are called *closet dramas* because they were never staged. Seneca did, however, greatly influence playwrights of later generations, especially during the Renaissance and Elizabethan times. Those playwrights borrowed many of Seneca's techniques: scenes of blood and horror, witches and ghosts, flowery language, and the theme of revenge. The violence in Seneca's plays reflected life in Rome during the Empire. He wrote about the crimes committed by tyrannical emperors and the intrigues in other countries.

THEATER AS SPECTACLE

Roman emperors wanted to keep the people's minds off the serious parts of life, and the large, unruly, uneducated masses were kept entertained. They had so many holidays that in 100 A.D. the Emperor Marcus Aurelius limited the number of holidays to 135 days a year. Sometimes there were 100 days in a row of entertainment. With often little to do, the people flocked to the Circus Maximus, the oldest and largest circus, to watch chariot races. Gladiators in full armor fought each other in amphitheaters. They were usually slaves, prisoners of war, or condemned criminals. The people yelled and raved during animal fights. They watched gladiators battle wild beasts including lions, bears, and panthers. Ultimately they watched unfortunate men, often believers in the new religion of Christianity, being thrown to the lions or other starving beasts.

The most famous amphitheater was the Colosseum, which could seat 55,000 people. Like other amphitheaters, the Colosseum was round with raised seats. Giant underground elevators were used to raise animals, people, and scenery to the ground level where they entered the arena through a tunnel. The amphitheater was flooded for sea battles, with

Inside the ruins of the Colosseum, Rome, Italy. Courtesy of Alinari/Art Resource.

ships holding slaves who fought to the death.

Audiences were easily lured away from plays to watch these spectacles. People demanded new and unusual entertainment. They wanted unbelievable effects like the 600 mules that were used in the play *Clytaemnestra*. The people loved bloodshed and violence. They expected actors to give real kicks and blows with their fists onstage. In the play *House of Fire*, a house was burned down. If a plot called for an execution, a condemned criminal was sometimes substituted for the actor and actually killed at the appropriate moment, to the delight of the audience. Playwrights tried to give the people what they wanted. The performances got worse and worse, horrible and indecent. But the playwrights and actors couldn't compete with what the people could so easily find in the Colosseum and at the Circus Maximus.

Christian Opposition

The leaders of the new Christian Church opposed and attacked the theater and its performers, especially the mimes, whose performances were often obscene and ridiculed Christian symbols and ceremonies. Christians called the productions "vile." Church fathers condemned the theater and exclaimed, "What tumult! What satanic clamour! What diabolic dress!" By the fourth century A.D. priests were banned from going to the theater. If you were a Christian and you went to the theater on a holy day, you were excommunicated—

banned from the Church. According to a council of clergymen who met in 300 A.D., actors could not receive the sacraments of the Church unless they gave up acting. In some places this was a law until the 1700s. If an actor wanted to marry a Christian woman he would have to quit acting. In the sixth century A.D., the senator Justinian had to persuade his uncle, the emperor, to repeal a law that forbade senators and actresses from marrying, so he could marry the mime Theodora. Four years later Justinian became emperor and Theodora ruled with him.

Other forces worked against the theater. Rome was invaded by a series of barbarian tribes who rode over the Alps during the sixth century. These Germanic tribes invaded and their leaders took control. Great upheaval followed; the Empire was divided. The barbarians despised the theater and eventually they suppressed it. The Roman theater ended in a shambles. We do, however, have the Roman playwrights to thank for much of what we know about the Greek drama and for their influence on later playwrights and theater architects.

The Dark Ages followed. There was no organized theater, no written plays, no formal stages. Actors traveled alone or in small groups from town to town to entertain wherever a crowd gathered. Storytellers, jugglers, and mimes carried on the theatrical tradition until a new age of theater dawned.

4. MEDIEVAL THEATER: OUT OF THE CHURCH AND INTO THE STREET

For at least the first four hundred years of the Middle Ages, often called the Dark Ages, there were no theaters built or new plays written for the stage in Western Europe. The last record of a stage production is the year 467 A.D.

Some of the performers who banded into small groups and wandered from town to town — the ballad singers, storytellers, jugglers, acrobats, rope dancers, animal trainers, minstrels, and mimes — performed in streets or public squares, wherever they could collect a crowd. Occasionally they were invited to appear at weddings, baptisms, and festivals. Priests who attended these events had to leave before the performers began their presentation. Minstrels, who sang songs in praise of heroes and warriors, were often welcomed in castles and the houses of lords because they provided entertainment and news of the rest of the world. According to one 13th century writer, minstrels needed to be skilled at card tricks, catching little apples on knives, imitating bird song, jumping through four hoops, and playing sixteen instruments. Some minstrels got rich as the paid servants of noblemen or kings, including Henry I of England.

THE CONFLICT BETWEEN CHURCH AND THEATER

Most performers during the early Middle Ages, however, were poor, lonely, and persecuted. The mimes who carried on the professional acting tradition banded into little companies of two or three people and performed simple sketches and dances in village streets. Often they slept beneath hedges by the roadside. They, like the other performers, were popular with common folk but condemned by the Catholic Church. Bishops and church councils issued many edicts against them. They even forbade acting. Church officials condemned the performers as beggars, thieves, vagabonds, and outcasts.

By the 10th century the European medieval world was held together by a common language, Latin, and a common religion, Christianity. Most people led a harsh life, but rich or poor, everyone accepted the power of the Catholic Church and its interpretation of God and of heaven as a paradise in life after death. The people prayed to God and hoped not to be tempted by evils they felt lurked in the world. It was the Catholic Church that took over many functions of government and tied Europe together. The Church was a powerful institution that had great influence over people's lives.

LITURGICAL DRAMA

It might come as a surprise that the most important theater to develop during the Middle Ages came from within the Catholic Church that had condemned players and their presentations for so many centuries. But the church did not use drama to entertain; it was very serious.

Liturgical drama, church drama, began simply. It began not as drama but as music, chanted words. These words, which were put to music and added to the Mass, were called *tropes*. The earliest trope for which we have a record comes from the Benedictine Abbey of St. Gall in Switzerland. It is known as the *Quem Queritis*, which means "Whom seek ye?" or "Who are you looking for?" It was sung in question and answer form by two

The Church of St.-Denis, France. Courtesy of the Metropolitan Museum of Art, Rogers Fund, 1922.

halves of the choir during an Easter service. This four line trope, which lasted for about a minute, relates the visit of the three Marys to Christ's tomb and their meeting with the angel who tells them that Christ has risen from the dead.

Late in the 10th century the Easter trope was acted, but the two choirs still sang the questions and responses in Latin. The *Quem Queritis* was dramatized by three priests wearing church vestments and veils, who represented the three Marys, and a fourth priest as the angel, wearing a church robe perhaps with wings. The church altar was used to represent Christ's tomb. Eventually more lines were added to the original text and then other scenes were added.

Another trope for the Christmas service was elaborated into a play. It began as a simple scene of the three shepherds greeting the baby Jesus and his mother at the manger, which was represented by the church altar. In Rouen, France five youngsters played the shepherds and a choirboy was the angel. Later a live ox was added to the scene.

Eventually the priests and choirboys wearing church vestments enacted other stories from the Bible. The Epiphany was another occasion on which a short play became part of the service to enrich the celebration. This play depicted the three wise men who follow the star in the East and present their gifts to the baby Jesus. Many plays became associated with the services during the Christmas season.

Some tropes never became plays. Some plays remained simple, with little action, and others became elaborate, with several scenes. Churches all over Western Europe produced one or two liturgical dramas a year, and the plays were always connected with a church service.

As some plays became more complicated, the priests used not only the altar but the whole, vast interior of the church or cathedral as the theater. The medieval church was built in the form of a cross, and aisles, galleries,

flights of steps, even the choir loft served as playing spaces. There were no pews or benches in the church, worshippers stood or knelt on the hard floor, so the wide empty central area or nave could be used as an acting area.

The different scenes were located around or across from this open area called the *platea* or place. Each scene could consist of a simple platform or a miniature house or room with no walls in front, known as a *mansion*. The platform or the mansion could hold small pieces of furniture like tables and chairs.

If you were a member of the congregation watching a play about the prophet Daniel, you would see three mansions — a royal palace, Daniel's house, and the lion's den — in different locations throughout the church or cathedral. The palace reveals a throne and a banqueting table; the house is just a simple framework structure; and the den contains a pair of choirboys costumed and masked as lions. As each scene is played in turn, you walk from mansion to mansion to follow the action. Sometimes the action spills into the platea. When a character moves across the platea, you know that it means he's journeyed from one location to another, or that time has passed. On other occasions the platea could represent a street, the country, or any space the play required. Even simple flying machinery was sometimes used to raise an actor, perhaps playing the part of God, to the choir loft, which usually represented heaven. Machinery also might be used to pull a star or to lower flames.

As time passed, the number of scenes increased so much in some cathedrals, and the settings became so elaborate, that the church drama was longer and almost more important than the worship service. At the Church of the Annunciation in Florence, Italy a platform representing heaven was erected above the church door. Here God was seated on a throne encircled by hundreds of lights and attended by children dressed as angels. In Pisa, Italy a globe was secured between two rafters of the roof of the church. Inside, on wooden brackets, stood twelve children about twelve years old dressed as angels with golden wings and caps. At the appropriate moment, they held hands and seemed to dance as the half-globe turned and moved.

Congregations continued to grow, people came from afar, and soon many churches were crowded with noisy and rowdy people during these yearly presentations. Audiences were sometimes so large that benches mounted on platforms were provided and placed in many parts of the church. This cramped the space in which the play could be performed.

PLAYS MOVE OUTDOORS

During the 1200s the clergy realized they needed to produce the longer plays outdoors. More people could view the action in an open-air space. The first outdoor location for the plays was the church steps. A platform was set up on the church porch or around the entrances to the church. Soon after, other locations close to the cathedrals were used, such as churchyards or a square near the church.

Over time many plays lost their connection to the church service. The dialogue was not always in Latin but in the language of the country where it evolved. Neither were the words chanted; now they were spoken. The actors might include laymen, and the local lawyer or farmer, as well as priests and choirboys. So, in addition to tropes and church drama, a new drama evolved. This drama could be elaborate, perhaps take several days to perform, and involved the whole community.

PRODUCTION OF MEDIEVAL DRAMA

In the 14th and 15th centuries much of the medieval drama was produced by nonreligious groups. In England and Germany trade and craft *guilds* produced and financed plays as their contribution to religious festivals. A guild was like a club, and craftsmen had to belong to one to practice their trade. In Spain, Italy, and France, religious and charitable organizations mounted productions. It wasn't unusual, especially in France and Italy, for guilds to be formed just to produce plays. These community groups would act in and secure all the costumes, properties, and staging needed to put on a play. In the most prosperous towns, where trade and industry had grown, you would find great dramas.

Although the guilds and other organizations ultimately mounted the productions, the church often supplied the scripts, approved other scripts, and watched carefully how the religious plays were presented. Craftsmen would make scenery, noblemen might lend costumes and properties, laborers could prepare meals, and priests might write out by hand all the individual parts for each actor. There was only one copy of the complete play text. If a hundred or more actors were involved, that number of individual parts had to be copied by hand. A medieval theatrical production was a monumental task, and the entire community was involved. York, England had a population of 5,000 people and 2,000 participated in the annual drama.

TYPES OF PLAYS PRODUCED

A variety of medieval drama was produced in cities and towns from Coventry, England to Lucerne, Switzerland. In hundreds of towns and cities with different cultures and different languages, annual productions of religious plays were offered. These plays provided a way to honor God, to glorify a city, and to teach the people — most of whom could not read — the lessons of the Bible.

The medieval plays were given many names: *mystery plays, passion plays, cycle plays, miracle plays, Corpus Christi plays,* and *pageant plays.* The miracle plays, with one or more episodes, deal with the lives of saints or martyrs and other religious stories not found in the Bible. A spectator at a miracle play might witness the miraculous deeds of Saint George or the life of the Virgin Mary. At another miracle play spectators would see the whole life of a saint, perhaps from crossing a sea and traveling through forests to battles and beatings.

Cycle Plays

The most spectacular dramas are the cycle plays — one-act plays grouped together and presented in order. The mystery plays are cycles — a series of short pieces — based on the stories of the Old and New Testaments of the Bible. If you watched a complete mystery cycle in England, you would see the history of the world from the creation of the world by God to the Last Judgment or the end of the world. The mystery cycle from York, England has forty-eight plays. Another cycle was the passion play, which deals with the Crucifixion of Jesus Christ on the cross and then his Resurrection. These were particularly popular on the continent of Europe. The English mystery cycles and the passion plays were the most important dramas to develop in the Middle Ages.

Many different types of locations were used to stage these plays. Cemeteries, quarry-sites, courtyards, even the ruins of Roman amphitheaters were used. A record from 1497 states that religious plays were staged in the ruins of the Colosseum at Rome. Besides the ancient amphitheaters, earthen amphitheaters or *rounds* were used. A round was a flat, round, open area surrounded by an earth embankment that was dug out of an open field. Raised scaffolds on the inside of the mound served as grandstands for the audience. Plays from the Cornish Mystery Cycle are still performed in a medieval round at Perranporth in Cornwall, England.

The most popular sites for staging plays were public squares and marketplaces. In Lucerne, Switzerland the Wine-Market Square was used as a theater. Today if you visit Lucerne, the square looks much as it did in the 15th century.

The sets for many of these cycle plays consisted of mansions on raised platforms set against a building or a row of houses. The stage platform might be long and rectangular with mansions made of wood and canvas set side by side on the stage. The mansions seemed to run into each other. The stage represented the entire universe. At one end was Heaven and at the other was Hell, with mansions in between representing several locations on earth — a temple, a palace, and the sea, for example. The mansions of Heaven and Hell were the most important since the plays were about the conflict between good and evil, God and the Devil. The arrangement and use of the mansions might change during the presentation of a play (one play showed seventy locations by the end), but Heaven and Hell were permanent. The open area in front of the mansions could represent one place and then another as needed.

Raised platforms weren't always arranged in a straight line. They might be erected in a circle, a semi-circle, or scattered about a rectangular village square. In German and Swiss cities where mansions were put up in a marketplace, wooden scaffolds to seat spectators could be placed up against the houses forming the square. Wealthy and important citizens watched the play from the windows of houses in the square. Sometimes people watched from rooftops. Often the common folk stood on the ground. When the action onstage spilled into the open area, actors would collide with the viewers. A performer playing the Devil often liked to run into the crowd and sometimes beat rowdy spectators with a padded club.

If you were a spectator, you would be awed at the sight of Heaven, a large mansion standing higher than the others, often painted in gold. Here an actor playing the part of God sits on a glorious throne. Behind him turns a huge globe with wooden angels or real actors

A modern production of the Cornish Cycle *at St. Piran's Round, Perranporth, Cornwall, England. Courtesy of Department of Drama, University of Bristol.*

Artist's interpretation of a Hell-Mouth. Illustration by Adam Broadbent.

A devil mask. Courtesy Tiroler Volkskunstmuseum.

dressed as angels. Branches of trees with flowers and all kinds of fruit—cherries, apples, pears, and grapes—decorate this scene. Birds are released. Ladders, cords, and pulleys are used for God and angels to ascend to Heaven or descend to earth during the course of the play. Clouds or cloud chariots suspended on wires or strings are used to make angels fly, too. Heaven radiates an unearthly glow, for everything is gilded, from clothing and weapons to makeup.

The mansion representing Hell would frighten yet excite you. During the Middle Ages people believed that they might be damned as sinners for bad deeds they committed and be sent to Hell when they died.

They hoped to go to Heaven. Sometimes Hell was represented by a mansion with an iron door and grating or by a two-story tower. In other productions, however, a *set piece* was built for Hell which looked like the gaping mouth of a dragon, monster, or toad's head with sharp fangs. This was known as the "Hell Mouth." The jaws could open and shut and clouds of smoke and fire spewed from the mouth. Creatures and devils with claws and horns, beaks and tails, bloodshot eyes and sharp teeth flew about and made horrible noises. Other devils might wear animal-like masks with cat features and leather costumes. Satan himself often wore a hairy coat and a horrible mask that belched fire and smoke.

Setting for the Valenciennes Passion Play, 1547. Courtesy Phot. Bibl. Natl. Paris.

Demons popped in and out of the jaws of the monster's head to threaten other characters or to drag sinners into the nether regions. Devils might even pop out of the monster's eyes, nostrils, and ears. In 1501 a production in Mons, France needed seventeen machinists just to work the special effects for the Hell Mouth.

Special Effects

Special and spectacular effects were an important and beloved part of the plays. In Valenciennes, France the life, death, and Resurrection of Jesus Christ was enacted in a twenty-five day production with a few hours of theater each day. Here spectators could witness the rod of Moses, dry and sterile, suddenly blossoming fruits and flowers. Other wonders occurred including water changing into wine, an earthquake, an eclipse, rocks splitting, and a fig tree whose leaves seemed to wither.

Animals were very popular, real or fake. In the plays about Noah and the ark, a dove was featured. Birds were used often, as were horses. Trap doors were needed for sudden

appearances and disappearances of characters. Trap doors or basins below the playing area were used for water effects, which were included in many plays. When the world was flooded during the Noah play, water might simply be suggested by a painted cloth or, as was done in Bourges, France in 1536, the platea was filled with water by diverting a nearby river. Real boats rocked on the water, too. Buildings were burned on stage, rain fell, and lightning struck in some plays, and real ovens were used in one production to bake bread.

Dummy figures were also used for scenes of torture and death so the performers would not be harmed during these scenes. If an actor in a play representing the life of a saint had to be burned at the stake, a dummy was used. It was filled with bones and animal intestines so it would give off a realistic smell. Dummies also might be tossed into real flames in the Hell Mouth or thrown through the air.

As a member of the audience at one of these outdoor medieval productions that could take from one to forty days to perform, you

Pageant wagon depicting the Annunciation, Brussels, 1615. Courtesy of the Board of Trustees of the Victoria and Albert Museum.

would see the whole story of the universe vividly set before you. You would have a better understanding of how God affects your life. There would be serious moments, sacred scenes, and comic moments and characters, too. You might particularly enjoy watching Herod, the king who rants and raves, who is out of control. The evil characters usually showed their bad behavior by shouting and convulsing. It was very funny. People loved to hiss and boo the villains. There were other funny moments. During *The Second Shepherd's Play* a man steals a sheep and tries to pass it off as his wife's new baby.

The Staging

There was a continuous parade of characters coming and going, with many of the actors remaining on stage in their mansions even when they had nothing to do. Often several scenes were presented simultaneously in different mansions and in the open acting area, the platea. In Valenciennes twelve scenes could be seen at once. The performances were on many levels too: scenes in the platea, in the mansions, and on upper levels representing Heaven and mountaintops.

If you were a spectator, you would constantly look from one area to another to watch the action as it unfolded. Or you might walk from one mansion to another to see each scene, if they were presented individually. Perhaps you stood or sat on hard benches for up to twelve hours every day. But, since such a production might be given only once a year (or two years or even ten years), you thought it was worth it.

Many of the cycle plays were staged a

different way. This method was popular in England where the plays were usually connected with the Feast of Corpus Christi. Imagine that you are living in the wealthy town of Chester, England during the 15th century. You've been excited for months, since the day you heard the town crier proclaim the name of the plays and the dates when they'll be produced. Early this morning, before dawn, you heard the herald sound the trumpet calling you and all of your neighbors to view the play from the streets. You watch the procession of important officials and the actors who will appear in the great cycle play. You stand in the street and soon the first play rolls up in front of you.

Yes, rolls up to you. Sometimes in England each play in the cycle was mounted on a *pageant wagon*. The wagon or cart was a high and large mansion on wheels. Sometimes it was open on top or on all four sides like a fancy stand at a fair. In other towns the pageant wagons had upright pillars that supported canopies with painted cloths hung from three sides. Often the wagons were two stories high. The bottom level could be curtained to serve as a dressing room for the actors. Sometimes the lower level was used for the Hell scene, with chains and fire. Simple pieces of furniture and properties would suggest the scene.

Other pageant wagons were elaborate. When the *Last Judgment* was presented in Coventry, England, the pageant wagon held twenty-five performers, the Hell Mouth, and a raised paradise for the angels. The pageant wagon for Noah's Ark was a large model of a ship. The actors could perform their short play on the raised mansion, or the wagon was pulled up to a scaffold or platform where the actors performed. Here the pageant wagon served as a scenic background.

After you saw the first play, you would wait for the next horse-drawn pageant wagon to proceed through the narrow streets of the city crammed with people and to stop before you. For each play in the cycle was presented in order at a number of stopping places in town — sixteen in York, six at Beverly, England. At each spot the actors would repeat their play. As wagon followed wagon you would see the whole religious history from the beginning to the end of the world. The procession of pageant wagons was like our modern day parade of floats. Once a year the city became a huge auditorium or theater. The whole community was the audience.

You would be tired after standing and watching the procession of wagons from early in the morning until dark. And you might live in a town where the cycle took several days to complete. Just as tired would be the guild members, for each craft guild was responsible for producing a separate *playlet* in the cycle. The production was the culmination of four or more months of work: building and decorating pageant wagons; making sets, costumes, and props; rehearsing and acting; and funding the playlets. Often each playlet in the cycle was assigned to a specific guild by the town fathers. For example, the shipwrights would present "The Building of the Ark" and the fishermen presented "Noah and the Flood."

Actors from All Walks of Life

The actors in medieval plays were remarkable. Most were ordinary men, perhaps a farmer, a law clerk, the town treasurer, men with no acting experience who volunteered to be in the plays. And sometimes almost anyone was taken for plays with huge casts like that in Mons, France in 1501, which had 350 roles. Young boys also were cast in plays, often to play the part of angels. In Italy some of the religious plays were presented entirely by boys. Men and boys played the female parts as well, although women and girls did appear in a few

of the religious plays in France.

These amateurs took oaths promising to appear on time at rehearsals, and they were fined if they missed or were late, unless they were sick. Free food and drink, cake, fruit, and wine during rehearsals and during and after performances was one enticement. There were other rules to follow. If for some reason a person couldn't fulfill his role, then he had to pay someone to replace him. After the performance, fines were given to a performer for not knowing his part or for playing "incompetently." A guild was fined if its play was considered "inadequate" by the town fathers. At Beverly, England the painters were fined because their production was played poorly and it reflected negatively on the whole community.

The amateur players were proud and committed, and they took their duty very seriously. The presentation of these plays was an act of devotion, another way to worship God. The honor of their guild and the pride of their town was at stake. In 1437 two actors, a vicar and a chaplain, became so engrossed in their roles that they almost hanged themselves during a performance.

SECULAR DRAMA

In addition to the incredible variety of religious theater during the Middle Ages, there was secular or nonreligious drama as well. *Farces, interludes*, and *mummer's plays* were just a few types. Farces are short plays with few characters, which show the faults of man and his ridiculous behavior. They are full of horseplay and exaggerated situations. In mummer's plays the actors, who were amateurs, entered the king's or nobleman's banquet hall disguised in masks and costumes, and the entertainment ended in a dance. Interludes, which were also performed privately indoors, were short plays with small casts and little scenery and dealt with a religious or political idea.

The people loved the street performers, the dancers, singers, jugglers, and the other popular entertainment throughout the Middle Ages. They enjoyed games, storytellers, sworddances, and other merrymaking. Mimes even performed in churches during the medieval period, although the clergy denounced them.

MORALITY PLAYS

In the later years of the Middle Ages, *morality plays* were popular as well. They were designed to teach their audiences a moral lesson while entertaining them. Usually a character representing man would be swayed and assailed by other characters who personified abstract qualities including Good Deeds, Justice, Death, Wisdom, and Folly. The play would show how man, the hero, is pulled this way and that by good and bad forces during his lifetime. Audience members could see how the Devil traps and baits people and how the Devil and Good Angel battle for men's souls. The most famous morality play is *Everyman*, which you can read today. In it Everyman, the hero, is called to his death. He asks Knowledge, Beauty, Fellowship, Kindred, and Goods to accompany him, but only Good Deeds will journey with him.

By 1600 religious drama had declined in Europe. The power of the Catholic Church had weakened when the new Protestant Church attacked its doctrines and suppressed them. Interest in classical learning revived, professional players found their niche, and dramatists started writing about non-religious subjects. Now, instead of Western Europe developing an international drama with religious themes, each country developed its own national plays.

We don't know the names of most of the authors of the medieval plays. The clergy wrote them and then they were rewritten by guild members. Many hands touched each script over the years. We don't know the names of the hundreds of townsfolk who performed in the religious dramas. But we do have the plays, and the medieval theater lives on through them. Many have been produced during the 20th century.

OBERAMMERGAU

Every ten years, high in the Alps in the Bavarian town of Oberammergau in Germany, *The Passion Play* is produced. In 1632 and

Oberammergau today. Courtesy Verkehrs-und Reiseburo, Gemeinde Oberammergau–OHG.

1633 the town was overcome by the bubonic plague. The people prayed and promised that if they were spared they would enact the passion of Jesus Christ, his hanging on the cross, his suffering and death, every ten years. According to legend, from the hour the vow was made no one else in the town died of the plague.

Every ten years since 1634 a large *troupe*, about 1000 of the more than 4500 villagers, divides the parts among themselves and plans the costumes, music, and scenery for the productions. They give about 100 performances in each year it is held. It is an act of faith and devotion that reflects the community spirit and support and the religious nature of the drama of the Middle Ages.

5. THE ITALIAN RENAISSANCE: GRAND STAGES AND DAZZLING SCENES

You are living in Florence, Italy during the 15th century and people, especially scholars and noblemen, are abuzz with a renewed interest in the classical world of Greece and Rome. Citizens are no longer as concerned about life after death, heaven and hell, their spiritual life. "Enjoy life on earth," everyone exclaims. Man is glorified and exalted for his own beauty and abilities.

ENTERTAINMENT FOR THE RICH

Italians read the words of the Greek philosopher Protagoras who said, "Man is the measure of all things," and take this idea to heart. Artists create for their own pleasure, not just to please God. Statues, palaces, paintings, royal processions, weddings, and plays—all are mounted, erected, and created on a grand scale. This is the Renaissance, which began in Italy around 1400 and later spread across the rest of Europe.

Florence was the richest city-state in Italy during the Renaissance. In the city-states, which included Venice, Pisa, and Milan, one family or the wealthiest families ruled and lived in beautiful palaces. There they founded their own academies and libraries and supported and surrounded themselves with artists and intellectuals. The wealthy encouraged the study of Greek and Roman art, architecture, literature, philosophy, all things classical. The rich thought the best, most cultured life was one modeled on the classical world.

Plays were presented at the courts of noblemen and princes but only as some of the many displays and entertainments mounted to celebrate an important event. A birth, engagement, marriage, crowning of a prince, visit of

an archduke—all required a lavish display. The wealthy felt responsible for cultural events. They also hoped to gain prestige, impress their guests (and the common folk who would only hear about the entertainments), and outshine other courts by mounting costly productions. As much as half a ton of gold was spent on a play that would be performed once and seen only by the rich people who attended.

When Grand Duke Ferdinando I married Christine of Lorraine, the couple and their guests enjoyed three weeks of festivities. The plays that were staged were only two of the events, which included a processional entry, a sumptuous banquet, a ball, the unveiling of a fresco, a concert, animal baiting, and jousting. When Grand Duke Francesco I married Bianca Cappello the guests enjoyed tournaments, the coronation of the new Grand Duchess, a hunt in the park and, finally, on the last day of the festivities, a play in the courtyard of the Pitti Palace. These entertainments were preceded by weeks of planning and creating by poets, musicians, costumers, scenic artists, and architects.

Among their many duties the court architects were responsible for creating stages, auditoriums, and scenes for the many entertainments. The architects erected temporary theaters in banqueting halls, ballrooms, courtyards, second-story rooms in palaces, gardens, and on an island. The wealthy Este family staged a play in 1573 at their pleasure resort, the island of Belvedere in the Po River. Garden stages had walls of clipped cypress trees and floors of turf. To build a temporary theater indoors, masons would see first if the space could handle the weight of a stage floor, sets,

Teatro Farnese, Parma (1618) Proscenium; designed by G. B. Aleotti. Courtesy of Archivi Alinari/Art Resource.

Teatro Farnese, Parma (1618) Auditorium; designed by G. B. Aleotti. Courtesy of Drama Library, Yale University.

machines, seating, and the audience. After the performance these stages were dismantled.

PERMANENT THEATERS

Architects also created new and impressive permanent theater buildings. They studied the ruins of the Greek and Roman theaters and eagerly read the long neglected manuscripts of the Roman architect Vitruvius. Then they attempted to copy the classical model and adapt it for indoor theaters. Instead they created a new theater. This theater, as reflected in the Teatro Farnese in Parma, Italy, became the model for our modern day theater.

The Teatro Farnese was built in 1618 in the sumptuous residence of the Farnese family. It still exists today, and if you visit it you will see its horseshoe-shaped auditorium with raised seats, a large open space, and then the stage behind a wide, permanent, sculptured *proscenium arch.* The arch is like a large picture frame that divides the real world of the audience from the acting area, the make-believe world.

TYPES OF RENAISSANCE DRAMA

The popes, noblemen, and other elite who were privileged enough to attend the theaters saw comedies, tragedies, *intermezzi, pastorals*, and *opera.* Scholars and writers searched dusty shelves in monastery libraries and great libraries, like that at Alexandria, Egypt, and rediscovered the neglected plays of Plautus, Terence, Seneca, and later the Greek writers. Audiences saw the original plays of these writers, then imitations of them and, finally, original plays written in Italian called *neoclassical dramas.*

Since plays were mainly presented on happy occasions, tragedies were not very popular. Many were based on Seneca's plays and contained much violence, horror, revenge, ghosts, and lots of talk, but little action. Most were poorly written. One writer describes

them as a "tissue of monstrosities."

The Italian writers modeled their comedies on those of Plautus and Terence. These comedies contained romance, kidnapping, intrigues, and the discovery of long-lost relatives. But it was the pastorals and intermezzi, and later opera, that the learned and aristocratic audiences relished the most. The pastorals let the spectators escape to a perfect countryside far from the real world, where life was quiet, happy, and simple. There nymphs and shepherds fell in and out of love with complications and obstacles brought on by satyrs and nymphs. Aristocratic women enjoyed acting in the pastorals.

The intermezzi drew louder applause than the plays. These comic performances with mythological and Biblical themes were given between the acts of other plays. Intermezzi dazzled the audiences with their music, dances, costumes, scenery, and special effects.

Opera, which developed in the 1590s, was the only original and lasting contribution the Italians made to theater literature of the time. It consumed and held the attention of Italian theater artists from the 17th century on. The Italians discovered the musical nature of Greek plays, so they invented a theatrical form that had dialogue and choral passages that were chanted to a musical accompaniment. This evolved into a form that relied on the music, more songs and arias, and on spectacular sets and mechanical devices.

WHAT THE AUDIENCE EXPERIENCED

Spectacles, lavish display, beautiful sets, and effects that surprised and dazzled — these were what the elite audiences enjoyed. When they entered the Uffizi Theatre built for the court of the rich and influential Medici family, the Grand Duke and his guests sat on an elaborately carved dais upholstered in dark velvet, which stood in the center of the open area before the stage.

The ladies sat on rows of plush carpeted steps which were set along three walls. Above these risers was a gallery with ten golden fountains, each topped with the statue of a boy. Myrtle blossoms stretched over the gallery and above this, leafy plants with fruit trailed. Fake birds perched on the plants, and live birds were released from baskets once the elegant audience was seated.

Seating the audience was done according to rank, with the prince or nobleman and his family always seated at a central spot in the orchestra — the space between the stage and the semi-circular tiers of seats behind. Ushers were careful to seat the ladies in the most important spots on the tiers according to their rank, age, and beauty.

Once everyone was seated, including lesser men on benches in the open area, the lights had to be lit in the auditorium and on the stage. The Italians brought theater indoors so lighting was important. The lights had to be lit quickly, too, so the audience wouldn't get restless or bored. Torches of white wax, oil lamps, and candles were used. They could be held in hanging chandeliers, in brackets on the wall, or in stands on the floor. Candles mounted in chandeliers just in front of the stage lit the auditorium. They were also placed at the front of the stage as footlights. Candles created less smoke and had a more pleasant odor than the oil lamps. Usually perfumes were mixed with oil to mask the bad odor. Often the lamps were used onstage where they rested on tall poles concealed behind the scenery. The torches of white wax didn't smell bad, but often they would get soft from the heat, droop over, and drip on the spectators. Unfortunately, the Italians had little control over how bright the light would be and exactly where it would shine.

The stage, framed by the proscenium arch, was concealed by a beautiful cloth curtain. Often to the loud sounds of music, drums, and trumpets, the curtain suddenly dropped and fell into the pit. The curtain stayed that way until the end of the performance.

SERLIO — THE FIRST SCENIC ARTIST

What audiences saw in temporary theaters and later in permanent theaters was influenced by the writings of Sebastiano Serlio. Serlio, a scenic artist, was the first, in his book *Architettura*, to set down the new principles for staging plays in private theaters. These principles were followed by scene designers in many countries for the next 400 years.

It was Serlio who first described how the Roman theater could be adapted for use indoors. His designs showed horseshoe-shaped seating — stadium-like seating for the audience in a rectangular hall. The front part of the stage floor was very wide and level but shallow. Here the actors performed. Behind this Serlio showed a raised, *raked* stage — a stage floor tilted up at a sharp angle to the back. From this we get our expressions *upstage* and *downstage*.

Scenery was placed on the raked stage. Painted houses or *flats*, created with light wooden frames covered by canvas, were stood and angled at intervals on both sides of the stage. They were aligned in such a way that they looked three dimensional. And they looked as if they went off into the distance, with the houses in front looking larger than those in back.

The flats were painted in *perspective*. Perspective allowed the scenic artists to draw objects on a flat surface and yet create the illusion that the objects were real. All the doors, windows, and ledges spectators saw looked usable, but they were only paintings on canvas. The buildings looked like you could walk into them, but they, too, were flat.

Serlio devised three designs for permanent sets, one each for tragedies, comedies, and pastorals. He wrote that these designs were sufficient for all plays, and his designs were imitated by many. For tragedy, marvelous

*Sebastiano Serlio's tragic scene. By permission of Department
of Printing and Graphic Arts, The Houghton Library, Harvard
University.*

*Sebastiano Serlio's comic scene. By permission of Department
of Printing and Graphic Arts, The Houghton Library,
Harvard University.*

Sebastiano Serlio's pastoral scene. By permission of Department of Printing and Graphic Arts, The Houghton Library, Harvard University.

palaces, massive columns, expensive houses, chimneys, and towers were depicted on painted flats. If you saw an ordinary street scene with city houses, an inn, a tavern, a church, and shops you knew you were watching a comedy. Windows in the buildings were made of paper or glass and lights shone through them. The "light" came from a lamp set behind glasses of colored water or wine, which rested on a board behind the windows of the painted house. During pastorals you would always see a woodland scene: trees with silken leaves, hills, country cottages, and rocky paths.

Eventually people wanted to change the scenes during the course of the play, especially for the intermezzi offered between the acts. Changing the scenes was always done in full view of the audience. It was considered part of the production and done to music. Viewers delighted in scene changes, especially when they were done smoothly and so quickly that they were hardly noticed. Many stagehands were needed to change the flats, back flats, and *borders*. For in addition to the painted flats or side wings, there were the painted back scenes, two large flats that met in the middle of the back of the stage, and borders, pieces of cloth that extended across the top of the scenery. These borders would hide lighting and special effects from the audience.

Stagehands could pull one set of wings off-stage because they were set in grooves. Another set of wings, a different setting, could be revealed. A later and more efficient system — the chariot-and-pole system — involved attaching the flat wings to poles which ran through slots in the stage floor. Casters (small wheels) were attached to the bottom of each pole and these ran on tracks beneath the stage, allowing stagehands to change the setting without being seen.

These settings, combined with the special effects, delighted the Italian nobility. The scenic artists and designers outdid one another designing and erecting complicated settings

and special effects. They vied to win glory for their court and to pay homage to their patron, the lord or prince to whose household they attached themselves.

IMAGINE YOU ARE THERE

Imagine that you are sitting on a velvet cushion in a private theater. You look beyond the auditorium into the vast stage behind the proscenium arch. A god flies through the air on a cloud. Now an entire choir and orchestra are lowered on a cloud that covers the entire stage.

In one intermezzo you watch sixteen boys who represent the wind suddenly appear from beneath the stage. They seem to fill the sky with brilliantly colored clouds by blowing air from their mouths. On each cloud you see a girl.

At another performance a sea scene is created. The Italians simulated waves by using long spiral cylinders which were rotated, one behind the other. Ships, whales, and dolphins move through the waves. This was achieved by mounting miniature figures on poles and moving them up and down from beneath the stage.

In another production you see a garden with orange and lemon trees. Perfumed water sprays over vine leaves twisted in trellises. Low hedges run along the ground. Suddenly the stage floor opens, and a mountain rises up with sixteen nymphs on it. On each side of the mountain moss-covered grottoes open to reveal nine characters on each side. At the end of the scene the mountain vanishes and the garden dissolves.

You also witness one of the most unbelievable productions when the Teatro Farnese opens in 1628, for here the auditorium of the second story theater is flooded at the end of the entertainment.

You barely have time to marvel at one scene before another appears. You see a mountain surrounded by clouds that drift up

A cloud setting in a scene from L'Unione Perla. *Courtesy of Drama Library, Yale University.*

and down. Flames shoot up in the background, and three figures rise upward and hover near the front of the stage. Later Venus appears on a cloud that transforms itself into a shell. And a sea appears from which a fortress rises and a silver drawbridge opens. Scenes flash by and then water rushes into the hall to rise to a level of one foot. Sea creatures made of wood swim by as do wooden dolphins and a whale.

A constantly flowing river, sea monsters spouting water, thunder and lightning, houses demolished, a scene in flames — all were possible. It is still amazing what illusions the scenic artists could achieve with cloth and wood and other common materials.

The actor was dwarfed by the stage machinery, massive settings, and the stage itself. The acting, however, was not important. Most often in this formal theater the players were amateurs — scholars, courtiers, even lords and ladies in the pastorals.

The actors' costumes were part of the stage decoration. Each actor was dressed very differently from the others and in a colorful way to present a striking picture. Actors playing servants never dressed in cheap or torn clothing. They wore satins and velvets. Performers playing the roles of the masters wore even finer costumes embroidered and decorated with gold and lace.

In one pastoral an actor playing the role of a shepherd was dressed in a bird's costume with real birds sewn on a white background, their wings painted in many colors. Often shepherds wore white silk sleeveless shirts covered with the skins of wild animals. Another actor playing a mythological figure wore a costume of bright blue silk with a panther skin across her chest. Blossoms and jeweled bees were attached to her hair and her headpiece of yellow silk featured a string of pearls and crystals.

The formal or intellectual theater existed for the pleasure of the wealthy. The great pleasure didn't come from the acting or the plays. The excitement and delight came from the more and more elaborate scenery, staging, theaters, costumes, and special effects. Although this theater was enjoyed by a small group, it did have an immense impact on theater for years to come. This theater produced many advances in theater architecture, settings, lighting, and special effects. It gave us the proscenium arch which is used to the present day.

Another theater, the *commedia dell'arte* or "popular theater" developed in Italy during this time. It was almost the exact opposite of the intellectual theater. The commedia also had a lasting impact, but a very different one.

6. THE ITALIAN RENAISSANCE: THE ACTOR'S THEATER

Noblemen and elegant ladies bedecked in lace gloves, diamond brooches, and gold belts applaud the comedy presented at the Este family's private theater at Ferrara, Italy. The greatest applause is for the costumes, 110 of them specially made for the five comedies given during these wedding festivities. Not far away, in the public square, an actor wearing a half-mask with a heavy nose and sly eyes passes a hat to collect whatever money he can from the standing crowd. These spectators applaud another comedy, a different type of Italian theater.

THE COMMEDIA DELL'ARTE

There were no frills, no elaborate staging needed for this theater. It succeeded on the skill of the performers, and audiences of all classes loved it. This popular theater of the Italian Renaissance was the commedia dell'arte, which means "comedy of professional artists." It was the first theater with professional actors who performed in organized companies, and it thrived in Italy from 1550 to 1750.

Commedia dell'arte troupes traveled from town to town asking permission to perform in the marketplace, in the public square, on a street corner, or at a fair. When they were allowed to play, the troupe quickly set up the portable stage they carried. The stage was a wooden platform on trestles with canvas scenery or a painted curtain for the background. The curtain or the canvas showed a comic scene of a street with houses. An area underneath or behind the wooden platform provided space for the actors to change their costumes. Only simple furniture, such as tables and chairs, and props were needed.

Sometimes wealthier commedia troupes rented a hall or a theater for a time. Noblemen and princes became patrons to some of the finest troupes, and the actors in these troupes could perform in the private theaters. There the troupes could take advantage of the elaborate scenery, the wings or flats that depicted rows of houses. But the commedia players didn't rely on these playhouses and settings. Their own abilities were what made the performances good.

Most of the plays of the commedia were comedies, for this was a theater of laughter. There were comedies that pointed out man's weaknesses and vanities. There were many stories about young lovers who try to get married but face obstacles. Greed and mistaken identities were popular topics, too. Many of the plots were based on the Greek and Roman plays, and other ideas for plays were taken from novels, local gossip, or current events.

There were no written plays, no scripts with dialogue. Instead, there were skeleton plots or scenarios that gave just the bare outline of the action. They indicate the actors' entrances and the sequence of the action. Almost 800 scenarios still exist in libraries in Italy, France, and the Soviet Union.

The head of the company, usually the lead actor, decided what situations the actors would perform. Before the performance this "director" would outline the plot for the actors and tell them the type of dialogue and actions they would need. It was then up to the actors to improvise the dialogue and actions, to make them up on the spur of the moment. The performers relied on teamwork. An actor had to respond instantly to the lines another player

Non,non,n'eftime pas en courant en barbet, | Ie fay l'arbre fourchu, portant les pieds en l'ær, | Dy ce que tu voudras, ie feray des premiers
En clabaut ou maftin,me rauit Frãcifquine, | Pour (difpoft) triompher en fi haulte conquefte | Au cõbat amoureux, que fur tout ie pourchaffe,
Ie veux eftre pendu maintenant au gibet, | Et toy plus l'ourd qu'vn Ours, ne fçaurois reculler, | Il n'eft chaffe en tout téps q̃ de bõs vieux limiers,
Si plus vifte que toyfur les mains ne chemine. | Ny aller en auant, tant tu és groffe befte. | Qui fçauët des cõnils le terroir & la trace.   iiij.

A *commedia scene (c. 1577)
with Harlequin and Zany
Cornetto. Courtesy of Drama
Library, Yale University.*

tossed him. The response had to be clever, and it had to make sense. It also had to move the action of the play forward.

Improvisation like this was possible only after much preparation. An actor or actress served a long apprenticeship, but hard work wasn't enough. A commedia performer had to have a quick mind, a rich imagination, a nimble body, and natural talent. Commedia performers were also expected to sing, dance, juggle, and do mime and acrobatics. The actor Visentini could turn a back-somersault while holding a wine glass and not spill a drop. Fiorilli, another actor, could kick high enough to knock his partner's hat off. He was eighty-three years old.

Performers could never "freeze" on stage or be at a loss for words. Players always needed a good opening for the actors playing opposite them so they memorized "stock speeches"—sayings, phrases, love speeches—that they could use in many situations. The actors studied hard and read poems, novels, letters, anything they might use on stage.

THE STOCK CHARACTERS

Each troupe had a set of *stock characters*—the lover, the servant, the old man, for example. These same characters appeared in play after play, and each character had a traditional name, a standard costume, a specific mask if one was worn, and a certain way of speaking and reacting to a situation. What changed from play to play were the circumstances the character faced and the different relationships in which he found himself. Usually, each performer in the commedia troupe played only one character all his life, and this time was spent perfecting the one part. Some performers gave their own names to a role.

In each troupe there were at least one if not two sets of lovers. The play usually revolved around the lovers' attempts to get married and the complications, misunderstandings, and jealousy that were stumbling blocks to marriage. The lovers' elders, fathers, old men, or guardians tried to thwart their plans, too, but the lovers stopped at nothing to get married.

The actor playing the *inamorato*, the male lover, and the actress playing the *inamorata*, the female lover, charmed the audience with their good looks, pleasant manners, and eloquent speech. These characters did not wear masks, and their costumes were the styles of the day. The performers could choose their own names for these roles, so the inamorato might be named Orazio, Silvio, or Ortensio and the inamorata might be Isabella, Flaminia, or Angelica. The commedia troupe also had two older men in the cast. They were often the fathers of the lovers and the heads of two households around which the play revolved. Pantalone, one of the old men, might be a greedy merchant, an angry father, a husband who is fooled by his wife, or a middle-aged man who falls in love with a younger woman. As soon as the actor playing Pantalone entered the stage, the audience recognized him by his costume and mask. There he stood in his black slippers, his tight-fitting red vest, red breeches, and stockings covered by a long-sleeved black coat. His head topped with a soft black cap bobbed up and down as he told his daughter Isabella that she could not marry Orazio because he wanted her to marry Silvio. Pantalone's mask revealed a darkish brown face with a hooked nose, a straggling, pointed gray beard, and a few wisps of hair peeking from under his cap.

When a character with black clothes, a white ruff on the collar, a professor's cap and gown, and a pair of gloves in his hand entered the stage, the audience knew that it was the Dottore. His dark mask with large nose, red cheeks, and short beard also gave him away. The Dottore was the other old man, Pantalone's companion, and often the father of a lover. The audience found themselves laughing at this medical or legal man who constantly babbled and gave advice about things he knew nothing about. The Dottore tries to sound intelligent, but he talks on and on and always gets his information twisted. When Pantalone is upset because his daughter is sick, Dottore suggests pills that are meant to cure a horse.

Another character who appeared in many of these plays was the Capitano. This swaggering braggart sported a moustache almost as huge as the large plumes on his hat. He might swish his enormous cape to reveal a wooden sword or gun. From behind his long-nosed and round-eyed mask, he boasted of his beauty, grace, and wealth, but almost always collapsed in fright at the slightest thing.

The most popular characters of the performance were the *zanni*, the comic-servants. They were the fun-makers, acrobats, and dancers. The zanni loved mischief. They might fool their masters or help or hinder the lovers in their attempts to get married. The zanni were lively and funny with their antics, tricks, and exaggerated expressions.

The many zanni used *lazzi* throughout the play to bring on the laughs. Lazzi or "jokes" were stunts, gestures, witty comments, and speeches that had little to do with the play.

In one play the character Arlecchino interrupts the plot by pretending to catch a fly in an elaborate and silly way and then eats it. In another performance Arlecchino pretends that his hat is full of cherries and eats them. Then he pretends to launch the cherry pits at Scapino's face.

Pulcinella, in yet another performance, is being escorted to prison when he tells his guards that he wants to tie his shoelaces. When the guards give Pulcinella permission to tie his laces, he bends over, grabs the guards by the legs, throws them over, and escapes. Lazzi that were popular were put into the *scenario* and used again and again.

The most popular and famous zanni was Arlecchino. He was easy to recognize with his black half-mask with wrinkles and his loosely fitting suit of many patches. Arlecchino also carried a small pouch with trash, stale bread, string, and torn handkerchiefs spilling out of it. Arlecchino wore a wooden slapstick in his belt, a wooden sword with a hinged flap that made a loud clap when he whacked Pantalone's bottom. Arlecchino evolved into the character Harlequin with his red, blue, and green suit of patterned diamond or triangular patches.

Audiences loved to watch Arlecchino, who would get an idea, plunge into a situation, and then try to wiggle out of trouble. He seems like a fool, but he has a quick mind and can always get out of a bad or embarrassing situation. He never learns from his mistakes though, and gets into more trouble or gets his master into a scrape.

In one play Arlecchino says he will kill himself because his love, Diamantina, doesn't love him. So Diamantina hands him a sword and a rope to kill himself. Now, what will Arlecchino do? It's not a problem for him. He talks on and on, making it up as he goes.

He tells Diamantina that he won't strangle himself because it's too vulgar. Then he picks up the sword, thinks, and declares to his love that he can't stab himself because it wouldn't be good to do it in his front or back.

Arlecchino had many companions, other zanni, who sang or played a musical instrument, often a guitar or lute. When the situation became confused, Pedrolino said, "Leave it all to me." Pedrolino became the sad, white-faced Pierrot in France. Another zanni, Pulcinella, became the hook-nosed hunchback Punch in the famous Punch and Judy puppet theater in England. Other zanni included Scapino and Brighella. The zanni had female counterparts — the *servetta* or maid-servants including Fantesca and the most famous, Columbina. They, too, were mischievous, witty, and helped in intrigues and trickery.

A commedia dell'arte troupe, probably the Gelosi with Isabella Andreini. Cliche: Musées de la Ville de Paris © by SPADEM 19__.

Here was a wild and energetic collection of characters in fanciful costumes and striking masks. Mix them up, have them confront each other, trip one another, and the play happened. There were surprising entrances, passionate declarations of love, lazzi, acrobatics, and phrases pulled out of thin air. Here is Arlecchino fighting a duel with Pedrolino because both want to marry Franceschina. There is Isabella dressed as a man so she can threaten and frighten Flaminia and marry Flaminia's boyfriend Orazio. This scenario or any other could be changed at a moment's notice to please the audience.

The performers worked especially hard for these audiences. They were a disorderly crowd, free to come and go, to pay attention or not. It was a challenge to entertain them. But the commedia performers were exciting, and even if a person saw the same scenario many times, he never saw the same play, for it was never performed the same way twice.

THE COMMEDIA TROUPES

Without the twelve to fifteen member troupes, this great theater might not have been. Constantly working together allowed all the members of the troupe to become extremely familiar with one another's styles and routines. A family was often at the center of a troupe, and many times members intermarried. The children in the troupe learned dancing and acrobatics as soon as they could walk. They were trained to take the place of their elders. In this way the traditions of the craft were handed down from generation to generation.

Commedia troupes had interesting names including *Accesi* (the Inspired), *Desiosi* (the Desirous), and *Fedeli* (the Faithful). The most famous company was the *Gelosi* (the Zealous). Isabella Andreini was a member of the Gelosi and the first great professional actress. She was a brilliant and beautiful singer, dancer, dramatist, and poet. Isabella also spoke four languages. King Henri IV praised her, medals

were created with her face on them, and one writer said of her "...while the world endures, while time remains,...every voice, every tongue, every cry will re-echo the famous name."

This was the first time in history that women held an important position in the theater. There were many other famous actresses, including Vincenza Armani, who were not only fine performers but learned, too. They studied the classics, science, and philosophy, wrote poetry, painted, sculpted, sang, and played musical instruments.

Troupes constantly wandered from town to town. The best troupes traveled throughout Europe in the 15th and 16th centuries. There are letters still in existence that show how the wealthy and powerful constantly commanded different troupes to entertain in their court theaters. They might even beg one ruler or nobleman to release a troupe so they could use their services.

The French court was especially fond of the commedia players. Henry IV and his wife Marie de'Medici requested the Gelosi troupe come to Paris often. Eventually the commedia players had their own Théâtre Italien in Paris. Even though the commedia troupes spoke Italian, they were understood everywhere because they used mime, dance, and improvisation so brilliantly. These techniques were a universal language.

AN INSPIRING TRADITION

The commedia dell'arte players and characters inspired and passed on their tradition to actors and playwrights in Spain, Austria, England, Russia, wherever they went. In England William Shakespeare used the character of Pantalone in his plays. In France the actor and playwright Molière was greatly influenced by the commedia actors with whom he worked side by side as a young man. The commedia had a great appeal, and it is still a living force in the theater today.

A contemporary commedia performance with Michael Fields, Joan Mankin, and Donald Forrest in Malpractice or Love's The Best Doctor. *Courtesy of the Dell'Arte Players Company.*

Many improvisation troupes and theater companies use the concepts of the commedia in their works. To witness a flavor of the commedia style, improvisation, and teamwork, you can travel to the logging town of Blue Lake, California to watch the Dell'Arte Players, who use lots of physical comedy in their plays. You can also get a sense of the commedia from The Road Company in Johnson City, Tennessee. This touring theater creates plays through improvisation, often plays outdoors, and includes juggling in their performances. Through these and many other troupes the spirit of the commedia lives on.

Joan Shirle and Donald Forrest in Slapstick *by the Dell'Arte Players Company. Courtesy of the Dell'Arte Players Company.*

7. THE SHAKESPEAREAN ERA: THEATER FOR THE PEOPLE

In the last half of the 16th century and the early 17th century, the English produced the outstanding and enduring dramatic literature that the Italians did not. But the English plays almost didn't get written, produced, or published.

THE PLAYERS VERSUS THE PURITANS

During this era the English followed the Protestant religion, not Roman Catholicism. Queen Elizabeth banned the medieval religious plays and cycles. Plays on nonreligious subjects developed, and actors played for profit without support of the government or religion. The Puritans, a religious group in England, thought plays were fine if they were religious and glorified God. However, they felt secular plays and acting for money and to entertain were evil. The Puritans cried, "The Devil is using the theater to lead people astray."

The Puritans badgered the government constantly throughout this period to outlaw acting and later, when they existed, to tear down the public playhouses. They regarded the actors as sinners and called them "caterpillars of the commonwealth" because they pretended to be other people. One Puritan minister condemned the playhouse as "the nest of the Devil and the sink of all sin." Others labeled the theater as a nasty sewer "whereunto all the filth doth run."

The mayor of London and the other administrators of the city were conservative men. When players came to London to perform their short pieces in the courtyards of busy inns, the city fathers were outraged and constantly made rules to get rid of the actors. The administrators stated that the plays corrupted young people, that youths saw bad behavior and subversive ideas portrayed on stage and then left the theater to imitate these horrible acts. Imagine what these government officials would say about some of today's television programs, movies, and music.

The city officials also warred with the actors over the afternoon performances, which they felt enticed people away from their work and from church services. They viewed the inn yards as meeting places for "horse stealers ...practitioners of treason and such." With so many people congregating in one confined space, the officials feared fights, riots, robberies, and the spread of the bubonic plague. The plague was a constant threat, dreaded by all Londoners. London was a crowded, unsanitary city full of rats. Fleas sucked the blood of diseased rats and then infected humans. In one week in 1625, 3659 Londoners died of the plague. So in times of the plague performances were forbidden in London. Often the playhouses were closed for months at a time.

THE INN YARDS

London was the center to which the traveling bands of players flocked when they weren't performing in village squares, in private houses, or at Court. In London a small group of players would arrange with the owner of a tavern or inn to perform their short pieces in the square open yard around which the inn was built. Inns, with such names as The Boar's Head, The Red Bull, or The Cross Keys, were surrounded by two- to three-story high balconies. From here the audience — people who had come to eat, drink, or lodge at the inn or

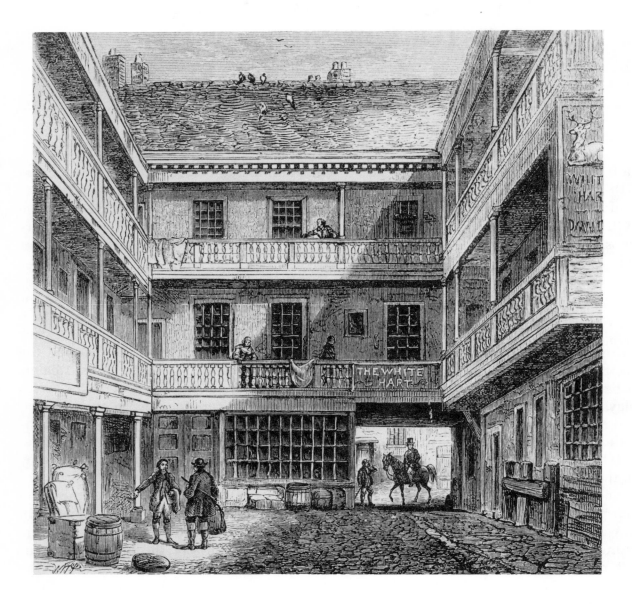

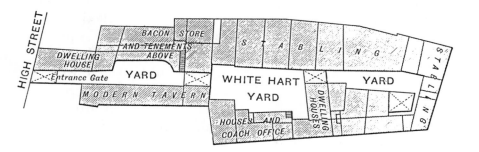

The White Hart: an inn yard for players. By permission of the Folger Shakespeare Library.

tavern—could watch the performance. They could also stand in the yard to watch.

The players simply set up boards on sawhorses or barrels to serve as a stage. This arrangement was convenient but not ideal. The owners of the inns and taverns didn't always grant permission for the players to perform. If they did, the players shared the playing space with acrobats, fencers, and bear-baiting, an amusement in which several dogs were loosed on a bear tied to a stake.

The inn yards were under the city's jurisdiction and we've seen how the officials regarded the players. In 1572 when Parliament, the government body, passed the "Act for the Punishment of Vagabonds" they branded the players as "vagrants, beggars, and vagabonds." The act stated that if the actors could not prove that they had masters—someone responsible for them—they would be "greviously whipped, and burnt through the gristle of the right ear with a hot iron." That was just for a first offense. Great lords and barons offered to be the patrons of some of the better acting companies and these troupes were protected from arrest. But the players received no financial support from the noblemen. While the strolling players struggled to perform their short interludes without being arrested or thrown out of town, a new English drama was evolving, but not for their use at first.

THE FIRST ENGLISH PLAYS

English scholars studied and imitated the ancient works of the Greeks and Romans which the Italian Renaissance brought to light. They wrote their plays in Latin and then in English. Later writers at London law schools and universities created a native drama by writing plays based on English history and with English characters.

Gorboduc, the first native English tragedy, was written by two lawyers, Thomas Norton and Thomas Sackville. The play relates the story of a weak king who lets his sons battle over the rule of the kingdom and how this decision leads to war. *Gorboduc* was seen privately at the lawyers' Christmas festivities.

The first native English comedy, *Ralph Roister Doister*, was written by Nicholas Udall, a schoolmaster, and performed by schoolboys. Most of these plays were performed by amateurs, university students, lawyers, and choirboys in universities, schools, and at the royal court. Many of these plays were written for the companies of young choirboys from court chapels and town cathedrals. They were trained to perform at Court or in private halls before educated and cultured audiences. The boy actors were very popular, especially with Queen Elizabeth. They traveled by cart and barge to perform at the royal palace, often enduring miserable midwinter journeys.

The finest groups of choirboys who acted were the children of Saint Paul and the children of the Chapel Royal. One of the boy actors, Saloman Pavy, who died at the age of thirteen, was famous for playing old men. Young Nathaniel Field was considered the second best actor in London, adult or child. The boy companies were directed by a choirmaster, and later by managers, who kept all the money the boys made. In return the boys received a good education. Some of the managers in the early 1600s kidnapped choirboys to be in their companies. One manager named Evans kidnapped a boy named Clifton while he was walking to school.

A PERMANENT THEATER

The English theater of this era might never have become great without the threats of the Puritans, city officials, and boy companies who offered competition for the adult companies of actors. Three factors helped the theater. James Burbage, a former carpenter and then full-time actor in the Earl of Leicester's company, built the first permanent professional public playhouse in England, a building erected solely to present plays. He called

Queen Elizabeth. By permission of the Folger Shakespeare Library.

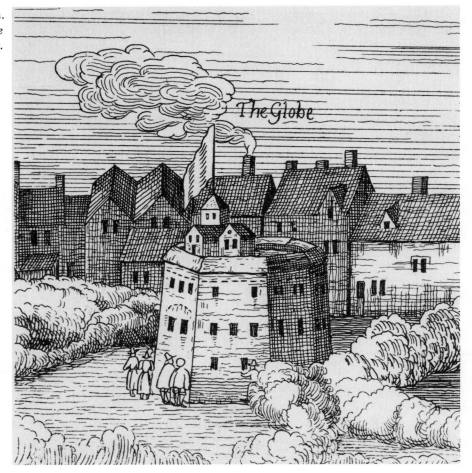

The Globe Theatre, London. By permission of the Folger Shakespeare Library.

his building The Theatre and located it outside the city of London in Shoreditch where the city fathers could not regulate it. Burbage knew that the city council had passed legislation regulating the performance of plays inside the city walls. The plays had to be licensed before they could be performed. This was in 1576.

Here in The Theatre players could collect money in a controlled way, hold a large paying audience, rehearse in the same space where they would perform, and build a collection of costumes and properties which could be stored. The company could afford to buy good plays to perform. They had a permanent home. Life was more stable, more secure. An acting troupe associated with a theater could earn a decent living and develop their craft.

Queen Elizabeth's Support

Queen Elizabeth and her court loved the theater. They looked forward to the actors bringing their best plays to Court every winter season especially for the Christmas festivities. There, late at night, in small, private indoor halls, the Queen and the aristocrats enjoyed the plays by the light of candelabra, tall candlesticks, and flaming torches. So each time the mayor of London and the city magistrates tried to close the theaters, Queen Elizabeth and the Court aristocracy stopped them. In 1597 a play was performed and immediately called slanderous by city officials. They ordered all theaters closed and the actors put in prison. Before this could happen the Queen intervened. The Court and the Queen protected all the public playhouses including The

Theatre, The Curtain, The Rose, The Swan, The Fortune, The Globe, and The Red Bull.

THE NEW PLAYWRIGHTS

The "University-Wits," poet–playwright–scholars who had attended the famous English universities at Cambridge or Oxford, changed their educated but formal style of writing and learned to write for the audience of the public theater. England was a great world power at this time. The English had a fierce national pride and love for their country. It was a time of Renaissance, too, a period when everyone was curious, adventurous, interested in learning. English people were eager to see plays on almost any subject.

These new writers, including Christopher Marlowe, John Lyly, and Thomas Kyd, pleased the audiences by writing a variety of plays on many subjects and in many styles. They often combined ideas from the Greeks and Romans with medieval ones.

Thomas Kyd wrote the most popular play of the 1500s, *The Spanish Tragedy*, which was called a "revenge play" because it contained a murder, ghosts, insanity, suicide, and a bloody ending, devices borrowed from the Roman writer Seneca. But the violence in Kyd's play was shown onstage. While Kyd's play showed this classical influence, it also ranged over many places and a long time span like medieval drama. Kyd lived out his own tragedy when he was arrested and tortured by government officers for his anti-religious views about Jesus Christ. He died in poverty.

Christopher Marlowe, a great poet and dramatist, also died tragically, at the age of twenty-nine in a tavern fight. Some people suspect that he was assassinated because of the spying he did for Queen Elizabeth. His was a tumultuous short life during which he was jailed for drunken violence and for his anti-religious views. But this rebel wrote brilliant plays including *The Jew of Malta, Tamburlaine the Great, Edward II*, and *The Tragical*

History of Doctor Faustus.

Each of Marlowe's plays centers on one character, one tragic hero, who struggles to achieve something more than he can ever hope to attain. Marlowe shows us what goes on in the man's mind, his inner conflicts as he challenges fate to get more than he can and then fails. In *Doctor Faustus*, the scholar Faustus goes beyond his place and seeks forbidden knowledge, sensual pleasures, and power unimaginable for humans. He makes a pact with the devil and then has to take responsibility for what follows.

WILLIAM SHAKESPEARE

The Elizabethans also saw the plays of the person considered the greatest playwright of all time, William Shakespeare. His plays have been published, studied, and performed in almost every country in the world from the United States to Australia, from the Soviet Union to China. Many professional theaters are devoted full-time to producing Shakespeare's works. The main festivals of Shakespeare's plays are given in three Stratfords (Shakespeare was born in Stratford-upon-Avon, England): England at the Royal Shakespeare Theatre, Canada at the Stratford, Ontario Festival Theatre, and the United States at the American Shakespeare Theatre. The New York Shakespeare Festival in New York City began a six-year cycle of Shakespeare's plays in 1988.

Shakespeare is the most frequently produced playwright in the world today, and only the Bible has been translated into more languages than Shakespeare's plays. His works have been adapted as ballets, operas, films, and musicals. *The Two Gentlemen of Verona* was an award-winning American musical. *West Side Story* is the musical based on *Romeo and Juliet*, which has also been interpreted as ballet, film, and opera. Shakespeare's plays almost didn't reach us. It wasn't until seven years after his death when John Heminges and

William Shakespeare. By permission of the Folger Shakespeare Library.

Henry Condell, actors with the King's Men, had Shakespeare's collected works published. Thanks to this book, the *First Folio*, Shakespeare's plays were preserved.

Shakespeare, the man, is a mystery; we know little about him. Even his tomb has strict instructions not to disturb his bones. We do know that he came to London for about twenty years, wrote his magnificent plays, and then left to return to the country. His plays were an instant hit with audiences, but critics regarded him as only one of many talented playwrights. Some fashionable people resented him because he did not have a university education or an aristocratic background.

Shakespeare was not afraid to take chances. With quill pen and parchment, he wrote thirty-seven plays of almost every type: tragedies, comedies, farces, chronicle plays which dramatized history, love stories, and fairy tales. He wrote four brilliant tragedies: *Hamlet, Othello, King Lear,* and *Macbeth.* In these serious plays the main characters are overwhelmed by unhappy, unfortunate events and ultimately suffer and are ruined or die.

Shakespeare also wrote comedies like *A Midsummer Night's Dream* about a girl in love with a young man who is interested in another girl who is chasing another fellow. Shakespeare's comedies usually involve love affairs full of misunderstandings and problems that end happily. In *The Taming of the Shrew* Katharina is "tamed" by Petruchio to be a suitable and obedient wife. *King John* is a history play about the king's efforts to keep his throne. In *Romeo and Juliet* two lovers' lives are ruined by a feud between their families.

Shakespeare explored a wide range of subjects. His strength was not in imagining original plots. Instead, he paid careful attention to the work of other playwrights, who had written many types of plays, and improved upon it. He took the revenge tragedy, for example, and wrote his own version, *Hamlet.* Shakespeare borrowed stories, plays, Bible tales, legends, histories, Greek tragedies, Roman comedies, writings in French philosophy, and poems, and reworked what was often dull or poorly written into something new and inspired. He took two of Plautus' plays and

A scene from a performance of Two Gentlemen of Verona by William Shakespeare. Photograph by Chris Briscoe of an Oregon Shakespeare Festival production.

A scene from a performance of The Taming of the Shrew by William Shakespeare, with Mark Singer as Petruchio and Fredi Olster as Kate. Photograph by Hank Kranzler of an American Conservatory Theater production.

A scene from a performance of King Lear *by William Shakespeare, with Peter Donat as Lear. Photo by Larry Merkle of an American Conservatory Theater production.*

A scene from a performance of Richard III *by William Shakespeare, with Randall Duk Kim as Richard and Megan Cole as Elizabeth. Photo by Hank Kranzler of an American Conservatory Theater production.*

created *The Comedy of Errors.*

Often Shakespeare used several sources for one play. *King Lear* was developed from history books, an anonymous Elizabethan play, and an Elizabethan novel. In *King Lear,* Lear rejects his daughter Cordelia because she won't say she loves Lear. His other daughters, Regan and Goneril, tell him what he wants to hear, but they don't mean it. Lear's pride leads to death and disaster.

Elizabethan audiences, like the Greeks before them, didn't need to see new stories, but enjoyed old ones, well told. In history plays Shakespeare dramatized the events in the lives of English kings, famous historical events, or ancient history. *Henry VI* (Parts 1–3) and *Richard III,* for example, dramatize the story of the War of the Roses, a chapter of English history the audiences would know. Like the Greeks they would want to see how Shakespeare would interpret these stories.

Shakespeare's writings are not like those of classical authors. His plays don't stick to one place or time or one line of action, and violence isn't kept offstage. The action in Shakespeare's plays ranges over long periods of time and through many places. *Antony and Cleopatra* covers twelve years and moves over the ancient world from Egypt to Rome. In *King Lear,* besides the main plot about the king and his daughters, there is a subplot involving Gloucester, who discovers too late which of his sons is true to him. Shakespeare also mixed comic and tragic elements, so in *Henry IV,* which explores events following the murder of King Richard II, there is a great comic role, Falstaff.

Elizabethans loved violence — hangings, beheadings, bearbaiting — so Shakespeare showed murders, lots of them, onstage. While watching Shakespeare's plays Elizabethan audiences were absorbed in fascinating stories, and they saw a wide variety of characters. There were passionate queens like Cleopatra, tormented heroes like Hamlet, characters of total evil like Richard III, jealous characters

like Othello. In addition to the kings and other rulers, Shakespeare's plays show us pickpockets, shepherds, generals, assassins, lovers, and drunkards. Elizabethans believed in ghosts, witches, and magicians, and Shakespeare included them, too. He offered something for every type of person in the audience. He knew that his plays would be seen at the public playhouses, at Court, in noble households, and at universities. He showed the whole world on stage.

Shakespeare's characters come to life on stage. They are fascinating people who seem real. They act and react the way humans do, in extraordinary ways and sometimes in ways that make no sense. They struggle the way real people do. Shakespeare didn't explain his characters, he let them go, and they come to life. Watching one of Shakespeare's plays gives you insights into human behavior.

Shakespeare knew how to build dramatic scenes full of conflict and emotion. His plays are acted regularly today because he wrote about conflicts and problems that still concern people, like hypocrisy, hunger for power, and guilt. Shakespeare created his conflicts, themes, characters, and plots with vibrant, poetic language. His dramatic poetry sets the scene and creates a mood, an emotion, an atmosphere. Ben Jonson, another fine playwright and Shakespeare's contemporary, said of him, "He was not of an age but for all time!"

Shakespeare's plays work well on stage because they were meant to be performed, to be seen and spoken before an audience. During this period plays were written not to be published but to last only as long as the actors wanted to perform them. Shakespeare enjoyed an advantage that playwrights in years past had not. He was an actor, a member of the Lord Chamberlain's Men, the most popular and successful acting company. They played at The Theatre and later at The Globe, the latter considered the most important playhouse of the time. Most of Shakespeare's plays were first presented at The Globe. As an actor in the troupe and part owner of the theater, Shakespeare knew the stage well. He knew how to keep a story moving, how to please an audience. He could write plays with specific actors in mind for certain roles. Many of his great male lead roles — Macbeth, Hamlet, Lear — were written for and played by Richard Burbage, the greatest actor of the time.

Many playwrights wrote scripts for specific acting companies. Each playwright knew who he was writing for, the strengths and weaknesses of the players. Playwrights found their work in constant demand, with many theater companies and audiences wanting to see something new all the time. Often just to keep up with the demand four or five playwrights would work on one play together.

THE ELIZABETHAN THEATER

As you recall, Greek drama was part of an annual religious festival, and the state supported the theater in Roman times. During the Middle Ages stages were temporary; plays were amateur productions with a religious connection, and they were performed infrequently. The theaters during the Italian Renaissance were either owned by noblemen or they were the makeshift stages of the commedia troupes who performed when and where they could.

The Elizabethan theater was different from all of these. The public theaters were owned by individuals, either by the members of an acting company or by a businessman who leased the theater to an acting company. Plays were held on a regular basis, almost daily, and the public could and was eager to pay to see professional productions at one of the nine permanent public playhouses.

As independent and in demand as the theater people of the time seem, they still had one obstacle to overcome before they could mount a production. Every play had to be submitted to the Master of the Revels, a powerful official of the Court. He was a special censor who read each play and looked for any words, phrases, or scenes that were indecent or criticized government policies or the Church of England. Some plays were returned with few changes; others had scenes sliced or so many lines scrawled over that the play couldn't be performed. If the actors performed an unlicensed play, the Office of Revels closed the theater. Sometimes the playwright and the actors were thrown into jail.

Finally, rehearsals were held. The theater company's bookkeeper kept the original copy of the play stamped by the Master of the Revels locked up, so no other acting company would steal it. In spite of the bookkeeper's efforts to guard the scripts, many were lost in fires or stolen.

The bookkeeper wrote each actor's part by hand. Then each actor was given his *sides*, a copy not of the entire play but of his lines and his entrance cues. The sides were written on a scroll which the actor unrolled during rehearsal. Actors didn't know much more about the play than their own parts.

THE ACTOR'S LIFE

With each company adding a new play about every two weeks and changing the play every day, there was little time for rehearsal. Each actor had to memorize quickly and keep many parts in mind at once. An actor sometimes arrived at the theater to learn that the play had been changed at the last minute. He might not have performed the play for six months, but he had to be able to play any work the company owned at a moment's notice. Some actors with small parts played two, sometimes six or seven roles in one performance. He might be a child, a soldier, a ghost, and a nobleman in one play. If you've ever learned one role, you can imagine trying to juggle five or six parts in your head at once.

Each actor always played the same role in each play. And the major actors specialized in one type of character. Also the actors could glance at the "plot" if they got confused or forgot something. The "plot," a sheet of paper dangling on a nail on the back stage wall, listed the sequence of scenes in the play, the names of the actors needed in each scene, the actors' entrances and exits, and the props they should carry.

Besides a good memory, the actor needed an excellent and clear voice to convey the playwright's beautiful poetry. He also had to be strong and physically fit. He might have to use a sword for duels or battle scenes or use acrobatics to leap off a balcony. The actor often had to dance in a play. Actors had to play an instrument, a drum or trumpet, for example, or sing, since music was an important part of many of these plays.

Actors underwent rigorous training in the dozens of theater companies, which consisted of ten to twenty-five men. The two leading companies were Lord Chamberlain's Men and Lord Admiral's Men. Richard Burbage, who played Shakespeare's leading tragic roles for Lord Chamberlain's Men, was a short and stocky man with lots of energy, who was hailed for his lifelike acting. Burbage was acting by the time he was thirteen. The other famous actor of the time, Edward Alleyn, created Christopher Marlowe's tragic roles for Lord Admiral's Men. He had a commanding presence due to his deep voice and his height, 7 feet. Alleyn was acclaimed as an outstanding actor by the time he was sixteen.

Famous or not, the Elizabethan players were always ready. Posters and handbills advertised the plays. Many people knew about the performances because coming attractions had been announced at the last show they attended. Also, a silk flag with the theater's symbol flying from the roof of the theater always announced a performance.

Edward Alleyn, actor. By permission of the Governors of Dulwich Picture Gallery.

THE AUDIENCE

The audience approached the theater by boat or over a bridge since the playhouses were across a river from the city. Workmen, young men from law schools, lords, bakers, businessmen, doctors, apprentices, families, household servants—all ages and classes of people—flocked to the two o'clock performance. They crowded through the door after paying a penny to the "gatherer" or "box-holder" who placed their money in a box and made sure no one sneaked in.

For a penny, people could stand in the pit, the open courtyard space which was sloped on an angle so everyone could see well. It was paved with brick or stones so people wouldn't have to stand in mucky soil after a rainstorm. The people who stood in the pit, often from the lower classes, were called *groundlings* because they had their feet on the ground.

Other people paid extra to sit on benches in the galleries or balconies, and some paid a bit more for the private boxes, which were special rooms near the stage. A select few paid to sit on the stage. The outside of the theater, made of wood frames and plaster walls, was either round, square, or many-sided. It surrounded a round courtyard open to the sky and was unlit and unheated. Most of the nine playhouses had three galleries with thatch or tile roofing, one above the other, surrounding the yard.

Peddlers mingled with the people in the pit and sold wine, beer, hazelnuts, apples, oranges, playing cards, tobacco, and playbooks during the performance. For a fee you could pay a young boy to crack your hazelnuts. Imagine concentrating on your acting while people crunch on apples and crack nuts.

As a player on the Elizabethan stage you would hear these noises, for the large rectangular platform stage with railings jutted out into the yard, and it was only about five feet above the pit. The audience, sometimes numbering 3,000, stood or sat very close to the performer on three sides. While they paid attention to the play, they were also enthusiastic and noisy and sometimes shouted and whistled. Players had to be very skillful to hold their attention and to concentrate on their parts.

THE ELIZABETHAN STAGE

A full skirt of cloth hid the under-stage space that was used for trapdoors and special effects like ghosts and graves. If you were a groundling at The Globe before a performance, you would have time to examine the stage. You'd notice that while you were unprotected by a roof, the stage had one. If you pushed up close and peeked at the underside of the stage roof, you'd see clouds, the sun, and the constellations painted on it. Then you'd know why it was called "the heavens." You'd also see the two wooden columns painted to look like marble that rose from the front of the stage platform to support the roof.

If no one pushed you back into the crowd, you could examine the back of the stage. There were two large doors which would be used during the play for the actors' entrances and exits and to move stage properties on and off stage. In some plays the doors represented houses, gates, or castles. There was also an opening between the two doors which was called the "discovery space." Here objects or actors could be hidden behind a curtain, revealed at an important moment, and then moved to the front of the stage. Behind the two doors was the players' dressing room, called the *tiring house*.

On the second level of the stage front, there was a gallery that hung over the back of the stage and served as an acting space. It could be used to represent windows, the walls of a fort, a castle, or a balcony. Part of it could have held the musicians and maybe some spectators.

You'd also see a half-roof over the upper gallery and atop the roof you'd notice a hut. Here ropes and pulleys and other machinery were housed and used for special effects like lowering gods or a hand clutching a burning sword sticking out of a cloud.

You've finished looking at the stage and you finally realize how chilly it is, so you put your hands in your pockets. Three blasts from the trumpeter in the roof hut lets you know that the play is about to begin. There is no curtain to open so you see the actors walk onstage. From the opening speech you know that this scene is set on a mountainside. You marvel at the young boy who is playing the main female role.

Boys played the female parts since women did not perform on the Shakespearean stage. Women in this era were not allowed to enter a profession; they could not get schooling beyond the basics. A woman was considered her husband's property and he controlled her life. It was felt that women didn't have enough experience to interpret the female roles in plays anyway!

The boy actors created some of the most complicated female roles. One, Edward Kynaston, was acclaimed as "a Compleat Female Stage Beauty." Foreigners who had seen women in female roles claimed that these boys played the female parts equally well.

A boy was apprenticed to an adult actor anywhere from the age of six to fourteen. He was chosen for his good looks, intelligence, and grace. Nicholas Tooley was Richard Burbage's apprentice. The theater company paid the adult actor for the boy's services. The boy's "pay" was his training as an actor. He learned to play a musical instrument, dance, fence, and to move and speak properly. The boy also lived with the actor's family who provided him with food and clothing.

A boy actor's life, like that of other actors, was not easy. He rehearsed in the morning, performed in the public theater in the afternoon, and then spent his evening learning new lines or giving a performance in a private theater or at Court. During times of plague he toured the countryside with the acting company. At the end of his apprenticeship, the boy actor might become an adult actor or enter another profession.

You turn your attention to the stage and hear a character describing the moonlight. You know from this that the action is taking place at night. Words, not scenery, were usually used to set the scene, to indicate the time of day, and to describe the location of the scene. Some plays used effects like those in the medieval plays — trapdoors, ghosts, gods descending, cannons firing during battle scenes.

Another realistic touch was the sponges of vinegar hidden in the actor's armpit and squeezed during a fight to look like blood. Bladders of pig's blood could be punctured during stage fights, too. The players used props and small set pieces like trees, thrones, rocks, city gates, and wooden hatchets. But the actors didn't use large painted backdrops like the Italians and the stage was almost bare.

In 1613 The Globe burned down during the opening of the play *Henry VIII*, when a stage cannon set the thatched roof on fire. One man's pants were set on fire and the flames were put out with beer. A second Globe was built a year later.

While there wasn't a lot of scenery, the English spectators marvelled at the actors' splendid and expensive costumes. Often the stage looked like an explosion of color: a peach satin "doublet" or man's jacket, glistening jewels, a blue calico gown, a cloak embroidered with pearls and golden thread, purple silk stockings.

The performers didn't try to make their costumes historically accurate. If they wanted to suggest that a character was from a far-off time or place, they used beautiful and costly fabrics. Roman characters wore Elizabethan clothing with a cloth draped over it. Ghosts, witches, and fairies wore fanciful costumes. Usually, however, the actors wore Elizabethan-style clothing. Because Queen Elizabeth wore red wigs the boy actors who played women's roles often wore red wigs, too.

A model of The Globe Theatre. Courtesy of James M. Stuart, President, Hofstra University.

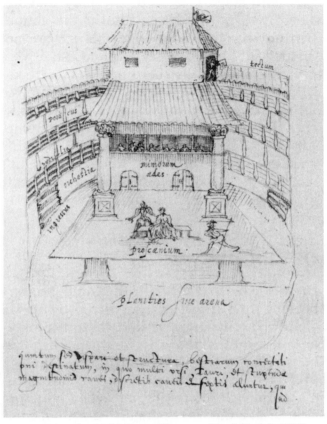

De Witt sketch of The Swan Theatre. Ms. 842, fol. 132R, University Library, Utrecht.

Sounds and music were integral parts of the plays. Bells pealing, thunder, cannon-fire, horses' hooves, fiddles, drums beating for an army on the march, trumpets to hail the entrance of a king—these were some of the sounds that filled the air. Songs were incorporated into many plays and music accompanied them. Musicians onstage also played for the dances in many plays and for the *jig*, the short music and dance piece that ended most plays.

There was so much for the audience to see and hear, and the play moved at a rapid pace, changing scenes as fast as a modern movie without stopping for about two hours. On the large empty platform stage, characters could march for awhile and the audience knew that time had passed and the scene had changed.

Or words could be used to change the scene.

A tent could suggest a battlefield where the actors shouted, waved banners, clashed swords. They could walk to another part of the stage, and the audience knew by the dialogue that they were in a prison. Later an actor would go through the back stage door, another actor would enter the stage, and the audience would be in another scene.

The play could "cut" from scene to scene by being played on several levels, sometimes simultaneously. In *Romeo and Juliet*, for example, Juliet could appear on the second level while Romeo declared his love for her from the main stage. Or a battle could be enacted on the first level while a scene in the besieged castle was played on the second level. Actors entering and leaving in, out, around, above the main stage level kept the play moving. There was no need to pause in the action. During Shakespearean times plays were not divided into acts and scenes, and there were no intermissions as there are now. Shakespeare's *Antony and Cleopatra* has forty-three scene changes, covers twelve years, and travels over the ancient world from Egypt to Rome. All was possible on this flexible stage, with the actors painting pictures with the playwright's words, and the audience's imagination creating the scene in their minds.

THE THEATER AFTER QUEEN ELIZABETH

In 1603 Queen Elizabeth died and James I became King. James was succeeded by his son Charles I. Shakespeare and the other playwrights continued to write for the public playhouses, but there were changes, too. James I preferred lavish *masques*, court entertainments that glorified him and relied on visual effects, like the spectacles of the Italian Renaissance. Much money was spent on these performances with male and female amateur performers. Prince Charles (later King Charles I) was one of the main performers in the masques when he was seventeen years old. Inigo Jones designed the sets, and Ben Jonson wrote the masques.

Ben Jonson also wrote tragedies, poetry, and his famed comedies including *Volpone* and *The Alchemist*. Jonson tried to improve people's behavior by ridiculing or satirizing human vices such as greed, foolishness, jealousy, and vanity. In *Volpone* the title character pretends that he is dying so he can get expensive gifts from people who think they can benefit from his death.

In Jonson's comedies or "comedy of humours," the main idea is that people's personalities are controlled by the four fluids or "humours" in their bodies. If one fluid dominated, the person wasn't healthy, but imbalanced. The person might be gloomy, mean-spirited, a fool, a hypocrite, or a villain.

Jonson was hailed as an intellectual, yet he lived a turbulent life. At times he enjoyed fame, but he was often poor and sick. During his life he was a playwright, actor, soldier, and bricklayer. Jonson was constantly in and out of prison for debts, fighting, and objectionable writings. He once escaped a hanging for killing an actor in a duel.

Other playwrights wrote during the reigns of James I and Charles I. The tone of their plays was different from that of the Elizabethan playwrights. Instead of plays about human nature and man's struggle, writers told stories full of thrills for their own sakes. *Tragicomedies*, serious plays with happy endings, were popular. Francis Beaumont and John Fletcher were a famous team who wrote tragicomedies. Instead of writing about real life, they wrote romances, dream-like plays that end nicely. Also popular were plays full of horror and sensationalism, like John Webster's *The Duchess of Malfi* in which a kind woman is destroyed by her brothers.

The adult professional players started moving into smaller indoor private theaters, lit by candlelight, like Blackfriars. Everyone had a seat; no one stood. Audiences here, where higher admission prices were charged, were smaller, more elite and upper class.

THE PURITAN REACTION

The Puritans, who had been opposed constantly to the theater, gained control of the government. Charles I had tried to gain control, but the people still wanted a voice in the running of their government, and they fought Charles in a civil war in 1642. The Puritans defeated Charles and beheaded him in 1649. They closed all the playhouses, forbade play-acting, and then tore down or burned many of the theaters. This was their revenge against the royal family that supported the theaters. Even The Globe, the most famous playhouse ever built, was torn down by soldiers to make

The Rose Theatre excavation. Copyright Museum of London; photograph by Andrew Fulgoni.

room for tenement houses.

Once again the actors were scattered and homeless. Some fled to France. Some determined players presented short farces in secret, but many of the illegal performances were raided. The audience members were fined on the spot, the actors fined or imprisoned.

Until recently it seemed as though the playhouses of Shakespeare's age were gone forever when the Puritans set torches to them. However, in March 1989 a section of the foundation of The Rose playhouse was unearthed. It was at The Rose that all of Christopher Marlowe's plays and many of Ben Jonson's plays were performed, and there Shakespeare appeared as a young actor.

Archaeologists have discovered that the stage was wedge-shaped and that the pit was raked—tilted up at an angle so people standing could see better. They have also found a leather sword scabbard or holder, odd shoes, a comb, and a human skull.

In October 1989 the theater world was excited again when three foundation walls were found of The Globe, Shakespeare's theater. Also uncovered were a Charles I coin and heaps of hazelnut shells left by Elizabethan theatergoers. It will be exciting to see what new information comes to us about the Shakespearean era as the digging and exploration continue.

From 1585 to 1642 the conditions had been perfect for an explosive burst of varied and rich drama and theater, probably the greatest ever for playwrights, actors, and audiences. The English writers of Shakespeare's era were the first to produce plays of lasting excellence, plays that would live on forever.

8. THEATER IN SPAIN: A GOLDEN AGE

The Spanish theater flourished from the mid-16th through the first half of the 17th centuries almost at the same time as the English theater. Like the English, the Spanish established a professional theater. During this golden age 30,000 plays were written, and the greatest Spanish dramatic literature was produced. Lope Félix de Vega Carpio and Pedro Calderón de la Barca, the major playwrights, continued to write plays even after they became priests. After Vega and Calderón no Spanish dramatists wrote significant works until the 20th century.

INFLUENCES ON SPANISH THEATER

Several factors worked together to stimulate and affect the growth and rapid rise of a national Spanish theater. Spain was a world power that controlled much of the New World, Mexico, Central America, much of western South America, part of the southwestern United States, and territories in Europe and Africa. Spain enjoyed a spirit of adventure, of pride and patriotism. Spanish explorers, soldiers, and adventurers sailed to America.

The Renaissance made Spanish people aware of their national history and legends. While other countries went through the Reformation and suppressed Catholicism, Spain was ruled by the Catholic Church. The Catholic religion was the moral and political force that united the Spanish people.

RELIGIOUS PLAYS

Religious plays, which were banned in other countries, were still produced in Spain. They were an important way to keep everyone's faith alive and to teach people the beliefs of the Catholic Church. Spain developed its own type of religious plays called *autos sacramentales* which were associated with the celebration of Corpus Christi, a feast day honoring the power of the Eucharist. The Eucharist is a sacrament in which, according to Roman Catholic belief, bread and wine are changed into the body and blood of Christ. The autos are like a mixture of medieval cycle plays and morality plays. Instead of showing Biblical stories and sacred events with just human characters and supernatural ones, the Spanish playwrights also included allegorical characters. So a Spanish auto includes God, angels, and characters that personify qualities like Sin, Jealousy, Death, and Beauty.

The Spanish religious plays differed from medieval religious plays in other ways, too. The Spanish religious plays not only included many comic scenes, they also incorporated singing, dancing, and spectacle, and the clergy approved. The best Spanish playwrights wrote autos as well as plays on nonreligious subjects.

The autos were staged on large, flat or two-story wagons called *carros*, moveable cars, which led to the Corpus Christi celebration also being called "Fiesta de los Carros" or Festival of the Cars. Like the English pageant wagons, the Spanish carros moved through the streets to each stopping place along the route, where the autos were presented on another wagon that served as a stage. The carros were beautifully painted, the actors wore exquisite costumes, and many carros had machinery for flying actors.

At first two carros were used for each play.

An auto sacramentale. Courtesy of University of Chicago Library.

Eventually four and then eight wagons were used. The carros were pulled from place to place by bulls or mules until this practice was banned because it was too noisy and disruptive. The autos also were presented at the public theaters and shown privately at Court before the king.

COMÉDIAS

Audiences enjoyed religious plays and the many nonreligious plays that were presented in public theaters. These secular plays, called *comédias*, were not just comedies, but any full-length play, comedy or tragedy. Comédias range in subject from mythological, historical, and pastoral themes to current social prob-lems, folklore, legends, and everyday life. Like the English playwrights, the Spanish ignored the neoclassical rules that said playwrights must limit the play to one time, one place, and one story-line, and never mix comedy with tragedy.

Characters in the comédias don't develop or change a lot during the course of the play. Spanish people saw the world divided into classes — king, noblemen, and commoners or peasants — and each group had specific rights and duties. Also the Spanish saw their lives closely ruled by the king, the Catholic Church, and a strict code of honor. This view was reflected in the plays of the day. There wasn't room for a character to choose his destiny, to deviate from what was expected of him, or to question authority. So what a character did in a play was more important than how he felt.

Another important facet of Spanish life, *pundonor,* was used as a theme in many of the comédias. Pundonor or "code of honor" motivates many of the men in Spanish plays. A man, as head of the family, is responsible for defending the family name and his personal honor. If a man's honor or reputation was attacked or tarnished, if someone insulted him or hit him, he was permitted to try to kill the person right then. If a husband's honor was blackened by an unfaithful wife, he was allowed to kill her and her lover. If an unmarried woman had an affair, she ruined the family honor and her father or brother could force her to marry the man, go to a convent, or kill her and the lover. Women were expected to live a modest and virtuous life and could bring dishonor just by flirting. Of course men could act as they wished and not lose honor.

Only through this violence and bloodshed could a man's or family's honor be restored. It didn't matter how the character felt about this code of honor. It was his duty to avenge any dishonor to the family's reputation. Audiences loved plays with action revolving around this theme of honor, and the French playwrights who followed were greatly influenced by this theme.

CAPA Y ESPADA PLAYS

The most popular plays were the *capa y espada plays* or "cloak and sword" dramas. These stories of love, romance, adventure, intrigue, and honor centered on the everyday lives of aristocratic and middle-class gentlemen. It was their clothing that gave these plays their name. They wore circular *capas* or capes that could be swirled or swung about to express emotion and passion or be used as a disguise.

The *espada* or sword was the other important part of the gentleman's clothing and was needed in duels to defend the man's honor or

to fling out to emphasize a point. Blend fair ladies and proud or jealous gentlemen with complicated love triangles, mistaken identities, characters in disguise, and people seeking revenge, and you had plays full of action. Usually they ended happily, often with everyone marrying whom they wanted.

LOPE DE VEGA

Lope Félix de Vega Carpio, sometimes called the "Spanish Shakespeare," wrote more plays than any other playwright of any time or place. Raised in a peasant family he wrote his first play when he was twelve and continued until he wrote more than 400 plays, some have said 1,800 plays. Because new plays were in such demand in his time, Vega sometimes wrote a play in twenty-four hours.

Lope de Vega wrote to please the public. He wrote all types of plays, pastoral, historical, many cloak and sword plays, and plays that revolved around the theme of honor. In *The Surgeon of His Honor,* a man suspects that his wife has been unfaithful. She hasn't and her husband knows it, but he feels that his wife must die to erase even the suspicion of dishonor. Lope de Vega was very popular in his own time. When he died his funeral was a national event with 150 funeral speeches that lasted nine days.

PEDRO CALDERÓN

Pedro Calderón de la Barca was an orphan at age fifteen. As a young man he was a rowdy soldier, but he went to university and upon Lope de Vega's death became the most popular Spanish playwright. He wrote more than 200 plays including many fine autos and comédias. His play *The Phantom Lady* is a good example of a cloak and sword drama. In it a widow, Doña Angela, falls in love with a guest, Don Manuel, who is visiting her family home. Don Manuel has the room next to hers, and he doesn't know that the rooms are connected by

Pedro Calderón de la Barca. Courtesy of the Library of Congress.

Corrale theater in Madrid, Spain. Courtesy of Drama Library, Yale University.

a secret passage. The widow sends secret letters to Don Manuel and enters his room at night. Don Manuel's servant is brought to her room by mistake. Doña Angela's brothers discover the servant and think that Don Manuel has insulted Angela's honor. The play almost ends with a duel but resolves happily instead.

Calderón's most famous play, and the most noted Spanish play, is *Life is a Dream*, which is still staged today, in 1989 at American Repertory Theater in Boston, Massachusetts, for example. *Life is a Dream* deals with the popular themes of pride and honor, duty to the king, and the question of life as illusion or reality.

THE THEATER AND THE AUDIENCE

By the time Calderón wrote plays, there were permanent public theaters, but the Spanish popular theater began with traveling players performing on improvised stages made of boards. The actor and playwright Lope de Rueda was the first head of a company of Spanish strolling actors that we know. It is said that Rueda carried all the company's properties — everything they needed to perform a play — in one sack.

The strolling players also could perform on stages in *corrales*, courtyards closed in by neighboring buildings. The corrales were controlled by religious orders of the Catholic Church that fed and clothed the ill, elderly, and poor and ran hospitals. At first the religious groups leased the courtyards of their hospitals to acting companies. Then they bought and rented corrales to acting companies to raise money for their causes. Finally, the demand for plays became so great that the brotherhoods built permanent open-air theaters in vacant lots. In Madrid, the capital city, the Corral de la Cruz was built in 1579 and the Corral del Principe followed in 1582.

Part of every admission fee a spectator paid went to charity. When some churchmen opposed the theater and actors, city officials and the religious orders defended the theaters because their local charities depended on the theaters for money. The city officials clamored for the reopening of the theaters for the same reason when King Philip II ordered all theaters closed for two years to observe proper mourning for the death of his sister.

The corrales and the permanent public theaters modelled on them were similar to the English inn-yard theaters, yet there was little or no contact between the two countries. England and Spain were enemies battling for control of the seas and seeking to explore and claim the New World.

Many theaters in Madrid were converted from existing trash-filled courtyards. Since the courtyards were surrounded by three-story inns or private houses, some of the boxes — private seating areas from which the people watched the plays — were located in private homes. The people who lived there either had to pay a yearly fee to use the boxes for themselves and their family or let high-ranking paying spectators walk through their homes to the boxes. Some boxes were rented permanently, and others were passed on to the heirs of particular families.

In the permanent theaters the side walls of the theater had boxes or stalls covered with iron gratings instead of windows from the rooms of surrounding houses. These were reserved for men and women of nobility and wealth. The area opposite the stage had a balcony divided from the other seating areas with its own entrance. This balcony or gallery was reserved for women, especially of the lower classes. Known as the "stew-pan," this gallery not only had its own entrance and stairway, but also its own peace officer to ensure that men didn't enter the area. It was considered important to preserve the women's honor. On occasion a man did sneak into the "stew-pan." In 1654 Bernardo de Soto slid in early and hid under the seats. When the play began he raised the ladies' petticoats and touched their legs. It created such a scandal that de Soto was banished from the city for two years.

The peace officer also kept the women under control, for sometimes they fought over a seat or a man. A woman who sat at the front railing of this gallery was considered shameless. She had come to the theater to be noticed by the men and to flirt with them by calling out to them. Men and women were not allowed to sit together. The only time a woman and man could sit together was if they were known to be closely related.

Beneath the roofed galleries in the courtyard were rows of seats raised like an amphitheater. In front of these was the patio, a large open space where men stood to view the play. In front of the patio and closest to the stage were rows of benches. There were also benches along the back and side walls of the building. At first some theaters were open to the sky, and people sometimes climbed to neighboring housetops and watched the play. Later the galleries were roofed and the patio was covered with an awning.

The *mosqueteros* were the spectators who stood in the patio. Many of these men made a game of trying to enter the theater without paying. They fought to get in free to prove that they were worthy of it. In Seville, Spain there were frequent fights and stabbings at the doorways of the theaters. Once a man fought to get in free and succeeded, rarely did he pay in the future.

The success of the play often depended on the reaction of the mosqueteros in the patio and the women in the "stew-pan." Playwrights and actors feared both groups and referred to them as *bestia fiera*, wild beasts. These men and women used rattles, bells, and whistles, boos and hisses, to show their disapproval of a play. They ate fruit, sweets, and thin-rolled wafers during the performance and sometimes pelted the actors with orange peels and cucumbers. On occasion the fate of a play was determined by one person. In Madrid, in 1679, it is said that a shoemaker, a nasty man with great authority, controlled the performance. If he blew his whistle or yawned, so did everyone else in the audience.

In some ways, the audience created the problem. They loved the theater passionately and wanted to see a new play every week. With such a demand, and with no one desiring to see an old play, dramatists wrote with such speed they had little time to perfect their work. And everyone wrote for the stage, including craftsmen, noblemen, and sometimes people who could barely read or write.

STAGING THE PLAYS

If the corrale and public Spanish theaters were similar to the English playhouse, so was the stage. The Spanish stage was raised, although it didn't jut out into the audience, and it had no front curtain. A curtain at the back of the stage could be pulled aside to reveal an inner stage that might represent a tent, or a bedroom, or any location. Curtains also hung from either side of the stage and actors could enter or exit from there. Behind the curtains was the dressing room. This was convenient. If a character was killed onstage, the actor could fall into the dressing room. A raised gallery behind the stage, like the balcony of the English theater, could serve as the walls of a city, a mountain, a tower, or the balcony of

a house.

Simple set pieces, trapdoors, magnificent and costly costumes that were the clothing of the times and not historically accurate were used as in the English theater. Even the staging was similar, with a change of scene indicated through words or by going in one door and out another.

The Spanish plays were unlike the English dramas, and the Spanish theater differed in another way from the English. Women performed on the Spanish stage. In 1615 boys were prohibited from playing women's parts and women from playing men's roles. This ruling occurred because the archbishop of Madrid felt that when boys played women's roles in female clothing it encouraged immoral ideas.

Actresses were paid as well as the men, and prominent actresses earned much more money than male members of the company. However, actresses had to follow strict rules. During this era in Spain women were kept in seclusion and only allowed out of their homes and on the streets if they wore a veil and were accompanied by a chaperone. Women could only perform onstage if their husbands or their fathers were members of the company.

In 1641 a regulation was passed that no woman over the age of twelve could act unless she was married. Women also had to wear decent women's clothing, a gown or loose overskirt that reached the floor. They could not wear men's clothing, wide hooped skirts, or strange headdresses. Spanish actresses were sometimes criticized for immoral dancing and daring costumes.

THE ACTOR'S LIFE

Between stringent regulations, criticism from the Church, and the will of the audience, an actor's life was not easy. Actors were paid only when they worked, and their costumes ate up much of their pay. Sometimes one-third of their yearly income was spent on one costume.

The Corral de Comedias de Ciudad Real. Courtesy of Tourist Office of Spain.

Often actors were in debt and pawned their costumes for money.

Slaves were considered to have a better existence than actors because actors were up at dawn; they studied from 5 to 9 a.m.; they rehearsed from 9 to 12; after lunch they worked at the theater until 7 p.m., and then they might appear at Court during the late evening hours. At least a slave had time to rest. The performers also spent a lot of time traveling from town to town.

Spanish actors did not have high social rank, and they had no civil rights. Most were recruited from the lower and middle classes. While they were rarely denied the sacraments of the Church, it did happen on occasion. Even in 1789 Cristobal Garrigo and Antonia Lopez Antolin were not allowed to be married by the Church because they were actors. In 1790 the actor Antonio Cabanas and his son were denied the sacrament of communion. And even though performers acted in religious plays, if an actor died in his profession he wasn't supposed to be buried in earth consecrated by the Church.

The Church resented the actors of the public theater for performing in autos sacramentales and religious comédias. They felt that often players who lived immoral lives played the roles of the saints, and they opposed this. Some regarded actors and actresses as people who perverted the public's morals and encouraged them to be lazy.

In spite of the obstacles and resentments against them, there were more than 2,000 actors during Spain's golden age. It is said that many common people adored the actors and actresses. They cried "Victor!" for a play they enjoyed. They even took scraps of the players' costumes home as souvenirs. The popular Spanish theater developed a wide variety of plays. People enjoyed going to the theater, and it was probably as popular as it was in England. The golden age of theater in France was very different from both of these theater traditions.

9. FRENCH NEOCLASSICAL THEATER: FROM TEARS TO LAUGHTER

While Elizabethans flocked to The Globe to watch Shakespeare's plays and the corrales in Madrid were full of spectators viewing Lope de Vega's dramas, the public theater in France stumbled along. Spain and England developed their popular national drama during the 16th century while they were world powers. At the same time France was in a state of confusion, rocked by foreign, religious, and civil wars. France had no great playwright, no permanent acting company, and only one permanent theater that was allowed to operate in Paris.

The Confrèrie de la Passion (Fraternity of the Lord's Passion) was an amateur group of performers who had been given a royal monopoly in 1518 to produce all religious plays in Paris. In 1548 the performance of religious plays was banned because Catholics and Protestants were debating the merits of their religions in the theater. The Confrèrie stopped producing plays itself but rented its theater to other acting companies. Any troupe that wanted to perform in Paris had to play at the Hôtel de Bourgogne, home of the Confrèrie, and pay a hefty fee for every performance. The Confrèrie usually managed to send away any acting company that tried to establish another theater in Paris.

THE INFLUENCE OF CARDINAL RICHELIEU

Cardinal Richelieu, prime minister of France who was considered the real power behind King Louis XIII, had a tremendous interest in the theater. In 1634 he allowed a second troupe, The Prince of Orange Players, to establish itself at the Théâtre du Marais in Paris.

With two permanent theaters, healthy competition began.

Richelieu was a learned man who decided to make France the cultural center of Europe. He wanted to be a great playwright himself. He protected and encouraged playwrights and actors, and this helped give actors greater status. Richelieu even passed a proclamation in 1641 that legally recognized *comédians* as citizens.

Richelieu believed that the French theater needed a dramatic change. He recommended that the French adopt Italian staging and scenery and had the first theater in France with a proscenium arch built in his palace.

These events happened at the beginning of the 17th century when political conditions in France became stable, and the theater had a further chance to grow. Richelieu's successor, Cardinal Jules Mazarin, continued his policies and when he died King Louis XIV ruled and he, too, supported the theater. Throughout the last half of the 17th century the King, statesmen, and the nobility controlled what happened to theaters and acting companies. Theater existed as a plaything for the court. The public playhouses were supported by the rich.

Since most playhouses were built and operated by royal permission, the royal court might suddenly decide to take a theater away from a company of actors. Or King Louis XIV might demand that an important playwright create a script with characters and a plot that he outlined. The King often commanded plays be written for the many balls, banquets, and festivals held at the theater at his Palace of Versailles which contained hundreds of rooms.

The King lived in the palace with all the

A performance in Cardinal Richelieu's palace, 1641. Courtesy of Musée des Arts Décoratifs, Sully–Jaulmes/Paris.

important noblemen. There and in the fashionable salons of Paris the aristocrats and wealthy discussed how people should behave and speak, what standards should exist for literature and other art. These people felt it was very important to observe proper social graces and the right way to do things. They liked order, rules, and laws. And proper appearance was crucial. Noblewomen wore jeweled gowns and high headdresses, while noblemen wore embroidered coats, breeches, lace, ribbons, bows, and powdered wigs.

The nobility and the bourgeoisie or middle class who imitated them weren't satisfied with the plays that were staged, mostly farces— comedies with lots of joking, horseplay, outrageous situations, and physical humor like characters chasing each other and falling off chairs. But a new drama evolved to replace the old comedies and Bible histories.

Scholars studied the Greek and Roman plays during this period of renewed interest in classical culture known as *neoclassicism*. More important, they read Aristotle's writings on Greek tragedy, set down rules for playwriting derived from Aristotle, and declared that all drama must follow these rules. Further, scholars stated, if a playwright didn't follow the rules his writing was immature. The men who judged plays were obsessed with these rules. The funny part is that the French plays written according to these rules were unlike the Greek and Roman tragedies.

These rules of playwriting were specific and numerous. Each play had to be divided into five acts, be written in verse, and observe the unities of time, place, and action. The "unities" meant that only one action, or main story, could happen in a single location in one day.

The characters in tragedies could only be kings and nobles, and the themes had to be important issues. Each play should be entertaining yet teach a moral lesson, show people how to be virtuous. Playwrights were expected to avoid anything that might shock the audience like obscene language or violent action, even things that were improbable or not true to life. Certain properties were considered vulgar, such as clubs and handkerchiefs. Yet swords, daggers, and poison were acceptable.

Only two types of drama were recognized, comedy and tragedy, and they were not to be mixed in the same play. This was the neoclassical ideal in 17th century France. William Shakespeare wouldn't have qualified as a neoclassical writer. He didn't observe any of these rules; most Elizabethan writers didn't. Neither did most Spanish playwrights. Only the Italians had tried to follow such rules, and they wrote terrible plays. When the French read Shakespeare's plays they were shocked. They called him primitive.

The Frenchmen who advanced these regulations for playwriting stated further that tragedy was the highest form of dramatic writing. Many French playwrights couldn't write any quality plays within these limits. Two playwrights, however, did write brilliantly within these rules, and they made French classic tragedy the best serious drama in Europe during the 17th century. They created a standard for serious playwriting throughout Europe to the 19th century. They were Pierre Corneille and Jean Racine.

PIERRE CORNEILLE

Corneille got into trouble with a play called *Le Cid* because he didn't obey all the rules. Audiences loved this play in which the hero Rodrigo must make the impossible choice between love for the heroine and defending his family's honor. The critics, however, were outraged. Cardinal Richelieu sent *Le Cid* to the French Academy he had created in 1635 and demanded a verdict on the play. The forty men in the Academy, which was created to decide what was tasteful literature, decreed that *Le Cid* was full of irregularities. Corneille was so hurt and shocked that he stopped writing plays for three years. Fortunately, he

Pierre Corneille. Portrait by Lebrun. Courtesy of Drama
Library, Yale University.

A scene from Le Cid by Pierre Corneille. Courtesy of Drama
Library, Yale University.

went on after that, but he obeyed the rules.

Corneille wrote many plays about uncomplicated, simple characters who become involved in complex plots. His plays, including *Horace*, *Cinna*, and *The Death of Pompey*, often center on heroes who chose death over dishonor. These heroes often find themselves in a no-win situation. They are called upon to sacrifice their personal desires for some higher cause or responsibility, perhaps to their family or country. But they call upon their inner strength and fulfill their obligation. In *Polyeucte*, for example, the hero struggles to suppress his love for Pauline so he can fulfill his duty to God by sacrificing all his earthly affections.

JEAN RACINE

Racine, an orphan who was educated on charity, did not emphasize plot. Many of his plays, such as *Alexandre* and *Andromaque* have little action. Instead, he wrote abut complicated characters and their inner struggles. Racine's characters are overwhelmed and controlled by their passions and they can't control them, no matter how they try. They wrestle with themselves, with their choice of duty over their desires, but their emotions win. Usually this ends in someone's death or destruction.

Phèdre, one of Racine's greatest plays, is about the Queen of Athens who struggles against her desire for her stepson Hippolyte. Phèdre knows very well what she is doing and how horrible it is to pursue her stepson, yet she can't help herself.

While tragedy was regarded as the noble form of drama, the comic writers were held in very low regard. That changed, due mostly to the efforts of one man, Jean Baptiste Poquelin, who took the stage name Molière.

MOLIÈRE

When Molière was twenty-one he decided not to succeed his father as the court upholsterer,

Elizabeth Hartley as Andromache. *Courtesy of The Billy Rose Theatre Collection, The New York Public Library at Lincoln Center, Astor, Lenox, and Tilden Foundations.*

the person who arranged the king's bedchamber. Instead he and a group of young actors who called themselves the Théâtre Illustre leased a dilapidated building in Paris and staged plays. They were a flop, Molière was put in jail for debts, and the group left Paris to tour small towns in France for fifteen years. They traveled on carts drawn by scrawny oxen and slept in haylofts or inns, two or three in a bed. They performed in the street and in wooden barns or stables with dirty rags as curtains. Sometimes the troupe enjoyed the patronage of a wealthy man like the Prince de Conti, and lived well. Molière and the other actors learned a lot during these years, especially from the commedia dell'arte players they met on the road.

The troupe was finally invited to perform at the King's theater in the palace at Versailles by the King's eighteen-year-old brother, His Highness Philippe, Duc d'Orleans. First, the troupe performed a tragedy, and bombed in front of the twenty-year-old King Louis XIV. Then they performed a comedy that Molière had written, and they were applauded. The King named the group "The Players of Monsieur" and granted them the right to act at a theater in Paris. Over time Molière made comedy as fine and important as tragedy in France.

Like Shakespeare, Molière was a man of the theater, comic actor, director, manager, and playwright. He wrote his plays with certain performers in mind including his wife and friends. Molière observed life around him and wrote about what he saw: the manners, customs, morals of the people of Paris. He observed the weaknesses, vices, and defects in men, and the foolish things that people did.

Molière wrote about and exposed greed in *The Miser*, jealousy in *Sganaralle or The Imaginary Cuckold*, and the pretentiousness of the ladies of society, who tried to dictate how everyone else should behave, in *The Affected Ladies*. Dishonesty, hypocrisy, vanity, injustice to women — Molière saw these traits in people and wrote about them in his plays. Molière wrote with humor and wit, and he created an array of characters including snobs, older men who chase younger women, and ignorant doctors. His intent was not to be hurtful but to be truthful, for Molière did care about people. Molière walked a fine line between trying to make the audience laugh at themselves, their peculiar habits, and their silly concerns, and having them resent him for what he wrote. Molière did offend people with his plays. In a society where so many people knew each other's personal and private lives, many men and women were sure that Molière was talking specifically about them in his plays. Often Molière offended powerful people. *Tartuffe* deals with hypocrisy in religion and a religious fake, and it was seen as an attack on religious groups.

Tartuffe was banned from the stage for five years. The clergyman Pierre Roules declared that Molière should be tortured in public. The archbishop of Paris threatened excommunication to anyone who read, saw, or performed in *Tartuffe*.

Molière never forgot that he was supported by the nobility. He considered himself a servant of the King and wrote plays and comédie-ballets whenever King Louis XIV commissioned them. It was the King who saved Molière and allowed him to continue his work in spite of attacks on his plays.

Today Molière's comedies are performed throughout the world, and he is heralded as the greatest comic playwright. But when Molière died in 1673 he was refused a Christian burial by two priests. Molière was suffering from tuberculosis and his friends urged him not to perform, but he worried that the other actors wouldn't be paid so he went on stage. He suffered an internal hemorrhage, choked on the last word in one scene, finished the show, and went home coughing blood. He had no time to denounce being an actor so he could receive the Church sacraments.

King Louis XIV intervened and ordered

Molière (Jean–Baptiste Poquelin). Courtesy of la Comédie–Française.

Molière as Sganarelle. Courtesy of Drama Library, Yale University.

the archbishop to bury Molière. Even then Molière had to be buried during the middle of the night, without ceremony, in a wooden coffin, and in an unmarked grave, in a section of the cemetery reserved for suicides and unbaptized children. Throughout the 17th century the French Church excommunicated actors and actresses. If performers didn't renounce their profession, they were called infamous and not allowed burial in holy ground. Actors often were abused and despised. It is said that Molière once entered the royal bedroom of King Louis XIV and offered to help the servant make up the bed. But the servant said that he wouldn't share his work with a comédian, and he left the room. In spite of this attitude, acting was popular and many performers did gain wealth, fame, honors, and grants of money.

THE ACTOR'S LIFE

Actresses performed in France, but they often were married to actors who were also members of the company. Usually the couple was hired as a team. Sometimes the actress was in demand and her husband just had to come along.

Actors and actresses belonged to one of the three permanent acting troupes in Paris: The King's Players, The Prince of Orange's Players, or to Molière's company. If an actress wanted to become a member of one of these three acting companies, she would perform in several productions. If the troupe wanted her, they would give her a regular salary.

When a playwright cast a new play, he decided who would play which part, and no one could refuse a role. Once an actor performed a role in a play, he was considered

A scene from La malade imaginaire *by Molière. Courtesy of Drama Library, Yale University.*

A scene from Le bourgeois gentilhomme *by Molière as depicted by Charles Robert Leslie. Courtesy of The Billy Rose Theatre Collection, The New York Public Library at Lincoln Center, Astor, Lenox, and Tilden Foundations.*

ready to perform it any time in the future, even three years later.

In a tragedy, the player chanted his lines in a dramatic and exaggerated way. The tragic actor Bellerose rolled his eyes and recited his lines in a sing-song. Montdory shook the walls with his "thunderous voice and gurgles." The tragic actor held himself stiff and erect, moved to the front of the stage, recited his lines, and then moved back so the next player could recite his lines. The actor didn't face the other performers or react to what they were saying and doing. There was little action or movement, mostly speeches, unlike the English and Spanish plays which had actors moving all over the stage, above it, and below it. Molière opposed this showy, exaggerated style of act-

ing with actors making huge and constant gestures and unnatural facial expressions. Molière trained his performers to speak and act in a more natural way. Few people preferred Molière's style.

Actors and actresses paid for their own costumes. They wore the dress of the day and bought the most lavishly decorated clothing they could afford. Fabrics were embroidered with gold and jewels. Women wore floating veils and high headdresses. Male performers generally wore long, full wigs that were considered fashionable for men. An actor portraying a classical hero wore the "habit à la romaine," a costume that looked like Roman armor complete with boots and a plumed helmet.

La Comédie–Française today. Courtesy of la Comédie–Française.

STAGING THE PLAYS

Many plays were performed in tennis courts. A form of tennis called *jeu de paume* had been very popular in France but was no longer. Many of the abandoned courts were converted into theaters by various acting companies.

The long, narrow indoor courts had galleries and balconies for spectators along two sides. Here sat the aristocrats and wealthy members of society, even members of the royal family. Merchants and professional men, even some noblemen, stood in the *parterre*, the large open floor space. The changing rooms for the tennis players were used as dressing rooms by the actors.

A row of windows just below the roof shed enough light for the performances. By adding a simple platform at one end of the long court, the troupe created a theater. It wasn't elaborate and many spectators had an awkward view of the stage, but it was functional.

Some wealthy spectators sat on the stage. They strolled on when they wished, talked loudly, and displayed themselves. There might be more than thirty spectators on stage, so it was hard to tell the audience from the actors. The actors might find themselves with a small sliver of space for their performance.

Permanent theaters like the Hôtel de Bourgogne and the Théâtre du Marais were not very different in layout from the tennis court theaters. The Hôtel was also long and narrow and most of the floor space was used for seating. This left little room for the stage.

The scenery for comedies and tragedies was simple. Since the plays were set in one place, only one scene was needed. The French, borrowing from the Italians, used two angle wings, wooden frames covered with canvas and painted in perspective, on either side of the stage. A shuttered backdrop, two flat wings that met in the middle, was placed at the back of the stage.

The curtain was raised before the performance, and the audience could look at the stage set with a few pieces of furniture, chairs, a table, and a stool, for example. The play began when the actors entered in the space between the wings and came to the front of the stage. At the end of the play, one of the actors would thank the audience and encourage everyone to come again.

Spectacular scenery and special effects, scene changes and ornate decorations like the Italians used, were enjoyed by small, elite audiences at the court theaters in palaces. Here operas and Molière's comédie-ballets were staged, as were *machine plays* that featured technical marvels like a sea of fire.

By the end of the 17th century, France had replaced Italy as the cultural center of Europe and was regarded as the leader in theatrical matters. By 1700 France's great period of dramatic work was over, but for another century they would set the standard for drama in Europe.

This great period did not end without the King intervening one more time in the theater. In 1680 King Louis XIV took the actors of Molière's company, who had joined the actors from the Théâtre du Marais, and he combined them with the actors of the Hôtel de Bourgogne to form the Comédie-Française. This theater, also known as the Théâtre-Français and the Maison de Molière (House of Molière), was the first national theater in the western world.

The Comédie-Française is still the national theater in France and has staged plays for over 300 years. It is considered an honor and a privilege to be a member of this theater. The Comédie-Française still presents the classical works, especially Molière's plays, from the 17th century.

10. ENGLISH RESTORATION THEATER: PRIVILEGED AUDIENCES, INDECENT COMEDIES

The Puritans, who in 1642 fought and won their revolution against the King, tried to eliminate the London theater completely. They closed and later demolished the theaters, banned the presentation of plays, and branded actors as rogues and vagabonds. Some performers went back on the road; others disobeyed the law and staged plays in private houses and inns.

Soldiers often raided and stopped these performances and confiscated the costumes. Actors who were caught were whipped or fined and thrown into prison, and spectators received the same treatment. It was a difficult time for theater people and a joyless time for most citizens in England under "Commonwealth" rule.

KING CHARLES II

In 1660 the Puritans lost control of the government and King Charles II was restored to the throne, so this period was called the Restoration. Charles loved the theater. He had escaped to France with many English courtiers after his father King Charles I was beheaded in 1649. While living in exile, Charles II attended the theater often.

Charles thought of theatergoing as a social activity, one that he wanted to continue in England. He became the chief patron of theater in England. King Charles and his court also brought back many ideas from the French theater. So many Elizabethan traditions were forgotten or discarded that a new English theater developed.

Charles II, known as the "Merry Monarch," regarded the theater as his property, his plaything. One of his first acts was to grant patents to his friend Thomas Killigrew (who played the part of a devil in many plays as a boy) and Sir William Davenant, a producer of operas. With the royal patents, Killigrew and Davenant each could own and manage a theater and acting company in London. By law these could be the only theaters in the city.

Killigrew and Davenant never forgot that Charles II was responsible for their good fortune, that he controlled what the actors did. Both aimed to please the King and his friends. The Restoration theater was not a place for everyone as it had been during Elizabethan times. The general public, many of whom distrusted playacting, regarded the theater as an activity for the court.

THE PLAY AS PURE ENTERTAINMENT

The audience consisted mainly of the King, who attended the public theater often, members of the court, upper-class people, and the fashionable men and women of London. These people, with too much money and lots of time, regarded the theater as a place to meet, gossip, or conduct business. They came as much to be seen as to watch the play.

Among the plays these fun-loving, well-dressed, and idle spectators saw were Shakespeare's works. Shakespeare would not have recognized these versions of his plays because they were heavily revised. Characters were removed, relationships between characters were changed, singing and dancing were added, two plays were sometimes combined, and endings were rewritten. For example, *Romeo and Juliet* was given a happy ending. Only a short time after Shakespeare lived,

Love for Love *by William Congreve as performed at Royale Theatre, New York, 1947. Courtesy Vandamm. Courtesy of The Billy Rose Theatre Collection, The New York Public Library at Lincoln Center, Astor, Lenox, and Tilden Foundations.*

many writers were trying to imitate classical French tragedy, and they were horrified by Shakespeare's plays, which don't obey any rules of neoclassical drama.

Other plays from the past were adapted and presented, too. New tragedies were written, among them *heroic dramas* in which a hero and a heroine agonize over fulfilling their love for each other versus meeting the demands of honor and duty to their country or family. John Dryden was the most noted writer of heroic drama. He presented the theme of love versus honor in such plays as *The Conquest of Granada* and *All for Love*, an adaptation of Shakespeare's *Antony and Cleopatra*. Dryden's plays were full of battles, horror, torture, blood, and sudden death.

THE COMEDY OF MANNERS

The most noted plays of the Restoration were the comedies, especially the *comedy of manners*. This type of comedy showed complicated intrigues between the rich and elegant members of the upper classes who lived in London. The characters in the plays were reflections, real or exaggerated, of the people in the select audiences. The court of Charles II was notorious for its immorality and "loose living." It was a society in which people were valued not for their honesty, morals, purity, or wisdom, but for their wit and cleverness. So the actors in the comedy of manners were elegantly dressed and moved and posed according to rules. They knew the proper way to handle canes and flourish handkerchiefs. The dialogue on stage was witty, intelligent, and full of word play. In these comedies everyone was a brilliant conversationalist.

The spectators enjoyed seeing their manners and carefree, pleasure-seeking life mirrored on stage, particularly in the plays of George Farquhar, George Etherege, William Wycherley, and William Congreve. Wycherley poked fun at the behavior and immorality of the upper classes. In *The Country Wife*, a play about a jealous husband who tries to keep his young wife from temptations in London, most of the characters are portrayed as fools.

William Congreve is considered the best writer of Restoration comedy. His works include *Love for Love* and his finest play and one of the best English comedies ever written, *The Way of the World*. It is still performed today. In this lively play Mirabell wants to marry Millamant, but Aunt Lady Wishfort opposes the marriage. There are deceits and accusations and a host of foolish characters. In the end Millamant agrees to "dwindle into a wife," but not before she declares in a clever speech her hope that she will be respected as an independent person and not just a subjected wife. In Congreve's time *The Way of the World* flopped, and Congreve did not write another play in the last twenty-nine years of his life.

The Plots

The plots of the comedy of manners were not meant to be taken seriously. One play might be about a young man's efforts to get rich by arranging a profitable marriage. Another play would feature two characters trying to work out a romance while one cheats on the other. In *The Man of Mode* by George Etherege, the hero Dorimant juggles three love affairs before he marries. Most of the plots revolve around the game people make of love and marriage.

The Characters

If you were in the audience you might see vain characters, hypocrites, greedy people, and flirts. There would be old men with young wives, old women trying to appear younger, and the "cuckolds," husbands of unfaithful wives. The "fops" would make you laugh. They are so concerned about their appearance and clothes, they pretend to be witty and polished, but they aren't. The main couple in many of these plays look at the people around them and try to mold a more lasting lifestyle,

not one full of temporary pleasures.

The other characters do live for pleasure and operate by their own moral code. Being good or bad is not important as long as people observe proper social etiquette. Everyone is, or tries to be, lovely, clever, poised, and privileged. And the characters' names reflect their personalities: Mistress Squeamish, Sir Courtly Nice, Sir Tunbelly Fashion, Lady Flippant, Sir Fopling Flutter, and Sir Novelty Fashion.

The First Female Playwrights

The Restoration audiences also saw the plays of several female playwrights. Katherine Philips was the first woman to have a play professionally produced on the London stage, and Mrs. Aphra Behn was the first woman to make her living as a professional writer. For a short time King Charles II sent Behn to Holland as a spy. Behn had a difficult time in the competitive, male-controlled English theater. She was resented as a woman, and her works and her morals were criticized, although she wrote the same types of comedies as the men.

KILLIGREW AND DAVENANT'S THEATERS

Since Killigrew and Davenant held a monopoly on theaters, it was their two acting companies who presented the Restoration plays. Killigrew's company was the King's Men or the King's Servants, who were considered part of the Royal Household. Davenant's company was the Duke's Company and their patron was James, Duke of York, the King's younger brother.

Killigrew and Davenant's first theaters were converted tennis courts since the Shakespearean theaters had been destroyed. Davenant's company ultimately settled at the newly built Theatre Royal, Dorset Garden, and Killigrew's company performed at the Theatre Royal, Drury Lane. Drury Lane has become the oldest, most famous theater in London. Four different Drury Lane theaters have been

built on the same spot during the last 324 years.

These playhouses shared similar features and set the pattern for English playhouses until the 19th century. They combined English and Italian styles and were small, rectangular, and enclosed. The theaters were roofed and the auditorium was divided into a pit, boxes or partitioned seating areas, and galleries or balconies.

The pit was a raked, slanted, U-shaped area filled with rows of backless benches covered with green cloth. People who came to be seen liked to sit in the front rows. The lowest gallery consisted of the expensive private boxes and extended around the walls of the auditorium ending over the left and right sides of the stage. There was a middle gallery and an upper gallery with benches for the poorer class of playgoers including servants.

Imagine sitting in one of the boxes over the stage. What a topsy-turvy view of the performance you would have. The King and the royal family sat in boxes opposite the stage, and this center position gave them the best view of the play. The middle and upper galleries were undivided, and here spectators sat on benches. For the first time every viewer had a place to sit.

The stage was framed by a proscenium arch as it was on the Continent. In England, however, the stage had a large open platform that extended in front of the proscenium arch and into the center of the auditorium. This platform was called the *apron*, and it was here that the performers did most of their acting. They entered and exited this area through two doors set in the proscenium. Actors could pretend that these "stage doors" opened into a house, bedroom, or closet. There was a balcony over each door called the "above" which could be used as another acting area. The area behind the proscenium arch was used for scenery.

The English used many practices from Italy and France. A painted backcloth hung across the back of the stage, and canvas flats

Eleanor (Nell) Gwyn. Courtesy of National Portrait Gallery, London.

painted in perspective were placed parallel to each other at either side of the stage. Sometimes sliding panels or shutters were used on the backstage. The flats were moved and changed along grooves on the stage floor and overhead. A new set of flats could be slid into view or one set of flats could be slid away to reveal another behind it. With this system a garden could turn into a bedroom.

The scenery was far removed from the performers and served as a background, a decoration. Each acting company had stock sets. For tragedy they had sets painted in perspective to depict a grove, a temple, a palace, and a hall. For comedy there were sets for a park and a bedroom. Since no attempt was made to suggest a specific location for any play, these sets were used over and over in many different works.

Imagine yourself as a lady or gentleman of the court. Since there are no reserved seats at the theater, you've sent a servant ahead to save a seat for you. You know that even though the performance won't begin until 3 p.m., the theater might be full by 1 p.m. And those people who do line up early might find lots of people inside who sneaked in through secret ways.

When you arrive at the theater you hand your round brass ticket to the doorkeeper and locate your seat in the first gallery. Throughout the auditorium people are talking and men are flirting with the ladies and the "vizard-masks," women of doubtful character who wear black velvet masks. You recall a recent visit to the theater in which several actors fought with spectators.

The audience were often wild, and the pit was the rowdiest place. In 1682 at Dorset Gardens two men argued, drew their swords, climbed onto the stage, and fought there. Sometimes men killed each other.

Today, however, the audience is calm. The orange girls are walking about the crowded pit, and you can hear them haggling over the price of the oranges, lemons, and other fruits they sell. Later they'll pass messages between the men and women in the audience. The head orange woman, "Orange Moll," supervised the orange girls. Mrs. Mary Meggs, "Orange Moll" at Drury Lane, was licensed to sell fruits to all customers except those in the upper gallery. They might throw the oranges at the performers.

Nell Gwyn, a poor child, was an orange girl at Drury Lane who became an actress when she was fifteen. Nell couldn't write but she could read her parts, and she played in comedies for six years until she became the mistress of King Charles II. During the Restoration actresses, often poor but pretty teenagers, were introduced into the acting companies in England. King Charles had seen and enjoyed actresses in France, and he issued a license in 1662 for them to appear in England.

THE FIRST ENGLISH ACTRESSES

When the first English actress appeared on stage, the theater managers didn't want the audience, who were used to men in women's roles, to be too surprised. So the audience was warned in a short speech before the play that an actress would appear. The English were delighted. They enjoyed seeing women in plays and were fascinated by the actresses' real lives.

Women brought insight into female characters, and playwrights wrote some brilliant parts for female characters because they wrote with particular actresses in mind. However, men still played the roles of comic old women and witches.

THE ACTOR'S LIFE

Players entered theater companies on a trial basis. They watched established performers and learned through trial and error. A beginning actor played many small roles, and after a few years, he discovered what types of roles he was suited for. Then he adopted a "line of business," a limited range of characters, for his entire career.

The actors often played characters unrelated to their own age. Some women played the part of Juliet in Shakespeare's *Romeo and Juliet* throughout their lives, although Juliet is a teenager. Actors owned their parts and once they were cast in a role, they always played it.

As you wait for the performance to begin, a young girl of about seven walks through the proscenium door in front of the curtain and introduces the play. Often, young children, especially girls, recited the prologue and epilogue of a play, the beginning and ending poem or speech that explained or commented on the play. Miss Denny Chock began reciting prologues and epilogues when she was six.

The prologue ends and then Thomas Betterton, the greatest actor of the age, walks onto the large apron. You are fortunate enough to see him in one of his best roles, as Shakespeare's Hamlet. Betterton is large and roly-poly. He has little eyes and stooped shoulders, yet he speaks with a powerful voice and his style seems more natural than that of other actors. Betterton doesn't act in an exaggerated way as many do. He is more restrained and dignified.

Betterton could play a range of roles — comic, serious, heroic, and tragic. In comedies his partner was Anne Bracegirdle, an excellent actress who was famous in "breeches" parts. These were roles in which she appeared in men's clothing. Bracegirdle was Betterton's pupil originally. Betterton was helpful to many young actors whom he trained and lodged in his home.

Today you're watching Betterton in a tragedy, and his leading lady is the beautiful Elizabeth Barry. Mrs. Barry, with her dark hair and light eyes, was a famous tragic actress who was noted for having an expressive face on stage. This was no small achievement. Most actresses kept their faces expressionless because they were afraid of cracking their heavy and stiff makeup. Their powder, rouge, and lipstick were applied over a layer of white

Mr. and Mrs. Barry in a production of Venice Preserved *by Thomas Otway. Courtesy of the Board of Trustees of the Victoria and Albert Museum.*

lead varnish.

As you look at the stage, you notice that the green carpet of tragedy is in place. You know that it is used to protect the costumes of the performers who must fall to the dirty and dusty floor during a death scene. Mrs. Barry's black velvet gown has a long train that is held by a page boy who follows her about the stage to keep the train out of her way. When she dies the page carefully arranges the costume about her. Of course, you and everyone else pretend that the boy is invisible.

A black velvet gown was traditionally worn by actresses in tragedies. In comedies women wore the clothing of the day, bell-shaped gowns of satin, silk, and lace with high-heeled shoes. They wore much jewelry, either borrowed or gifts from admirers and, in general, looked gorgeous from afar. Close up they looked gaudy, almost frightening. Men usually wore current fashions, too — jackets embroidered with silver and gold with wide cuffs and pockets that hung low. Lace and ribbon trimmed their shirts, breeches, and stockings. They also wore high-heeled shoes and carried accessories like gloves and muffs. Their costumes were completed by wigs of long hair that fell over the actors' shoulders and tumbled down their backs.

You aren't watching the actors now because the stagehands are changing the scenery. You watch the new set of shutters as it slides in front of the panels from the last scene. Chairs, tables, and books are painted on the flats.

Because furniture is rarely used on stage, the performers stand throughout the play. They stand close to the edge of the stage to be heard and to control the restless audience. All the performers and their pages stay on stage throughout the play and whisper, look around, or bow to friends in the audience.

THE PERFORMANCE

You enjoy the songs and musical interludes during the scene change and the dancing of a little girl. The musicians seated in a gallery above the stage play a variety of instruments including an oboe, a bassoon, a flute, and a mandolin.

You also look at the audience. This is easy to do as the auditorium and the stage are brightly lit by chandeliers of candles during the entire performance. Footlights are used, too. This innovation consists of a short strip of candles floating in a shallow tray of water or oil lamps at the edge of the stage. Colored lights are created by placing strips of colored silk in front of the candles and lamps.

A fire could start any time with this lighting system, so candle snuffers stood close by to attend to the candles. If a candle started to sputter, the snuffer or attendant would walk on stage and correct the problem. These attendants ignored the actors and were regarded as invisible by the audience.

As the performance progresses, you become aware of the glare and heat of the candles. It's almost like a furnace in the auditorium. The candles, made of mutton fat, give off obnoxious fumes and create a haze of smoke. The smell mingles with the stench from the communal toilets in the passageways behind the galleries and the odors of unwashed bodies since people don't bathe often. No wonder men and women wear perfume and sniff pomanders or snuff.

In spite of these discomforts and the noisy and rowdy audience, you enjoy the performance and get to chat with several friends. When the play ends an actor comes out and announces the show for the next day. People don't leave right away. They stay at the theater to gossip, criticize the drama they've seen, or pay to talk to the actresses in their dressing rooms.

As the coach takes you home along tree-lined roads, you daydream about joining a Nursery — a training school for young actors. Sometimes the students perform in productions. Upon graduation you become a member of an acting company in London, or you join a touring company in the country. You are having this daydream at the end of the 17th century when many things are about to change in the English theater.

THE END OF AN ERA

In 1685 the death of Charles II had a huge effect on the theater. Charles had tolerated coarse and risqué plays. He had allowed players and playwrights to do what they wanted in comedies, and the results were not always tasteful.

In 1698 the Reverend Jeremy Collier published a now famous attack on the Restoration theater. In his pamphlet, *A Short View of the Immorality and Profaneness of the English Stage*, Collier said the Restoration plays were "faulty to a scandalous degree of nauseousness. . . ." The kings and queens who followed King Charles, William and Mary and Queen Anne, wanted the public to behave in a less frivolous and more moral way. A new middle class was rising and they wanted dramas that reflected their morals, not those of the Court. The next century would see a very different drama and audience in the English theater.

11. ASIA:
A DIFFERENT THEATER TRADITION

While the theater in Europe was evolving, Asia was independently developing its own unique theater. In this theater, music, song, dance, speech, gestures, and acting are important, and all are combined to create a performance. It was not until the middle of the 18th century, however, that the Eastern theater began to influence theater in the West.

THEATER IN INDIA

India was the first Asian country to develop its theater. The classical drama of India grew out of a religious observance and was performed at a festival or public celebration. A king or a wealthy nobleman would summon a group of actors to perform in a temple, or at the palace in a specially adapted room or garden. The audience consisted of the nobility, the upper classes, the king, and his courtiers.

On a simple platform stage with little or no scenery, the highly trained actors appeared in splendid, symbolic costumes. They sang to the accompaniment of drums and stringed instruments and used dance, mime, and a language of gestures to tell their story.

The gods are main characters in many of these classical dramas. Most of these dramas are based on history, legends, and on two long epic poems about the adventures of Indian gods and heroes, Ramayana and Mahabharata. These works contain hundreds of gods, devils, kings, ogres, heroes, and heroines, so the plays are about these characters. Love and romance is the subject of many of these plays, as is good versus evil. These dramas have happy endings and the hero always wins.

Indian Playwriting

Indian playwriting had its "golden age" in the fourth and fifth centuries. The playwrights were concerned more with creating a feeling than developing a story or plot. Each play is developed around one of nine *rasas*, meaning "flavor" or mood, and including love, sorrow, anger, horror, and wonder. The playwrights were aware always of taboos and never included kissing, scratching, biting, eating, or sleeping in their plays.

The greatest poet and dramatist of India during this classical age, which peaked in 700 A.D., was Kalidasa. His play *Shakuntala or The Recovered Ring*, written in 400 A.D., is the greatest drama from this age. It is a tale of two long parted lovers who are happily reunited. Another play from this age, *The Little Clay Cart*, is about love, intrigue, and jealousy. Both of these plays have been produced in the West in the 20th century. *The Little Clay Cart* was staged in New York City in 1924 and in London, England in 1964.

Indian folk drama existed during the classical age and continues to flourish today in 700,000 towns and villages in India. Romance and the conflict between the gods and demons are popular subjects for this theater of the people. There are many types of folk drama, but most take place in marketplaces, street corners, country fairs, and courtyards of temples. A temporary raised platform is used, and the setting is simple. Sometimes large canopy-like tents decorated with flowers and leaves are used or bamboo structures are built. The performances usually begin between 8 and 10 p.m. and last late into the night.

Kathakali, South Indian dance drama. Courtesy of The Asia Society.

Kathakali, South Indian dance drama. Courtesy of The Asia Society.

Kathakali

Today, in Kerala, the southwest tip of India, a stylized dance-drama called *Kathakali* is very popular. It is one of the hundreds of folk theaters that exists in India. The characters are gods, demons, heroes, heroines, and supernatural beings. The stories are well-known to the audience gathered under the stars to watch the performances by torchlight.

Much happens before the performance begins. Early in the morning the actor lies face down on the ground wearing a loincloth. A man massages, kneads, and slaps the actor's back with his feet. Then the actor lies on his back while makeup men build a half-inch thick frame on his face consisting of layers of rice paste and paper that hardens like plaster of Paris. Colorful and elaborate designs that represent a specific character are painted on the actor's face. During the five-hour makeup session, the actor can't move any part of his face.

The actor then takes a long time to put on his elaborate costume. Layers of clothing are put on: enormous hoop skirts cover the lower part of the body. There are jackets, scarves, plumes, long silver nails on the fingers of the left hand, red and gold discs to cover the ears, and ancient jewelry. Finally the actor dons a waist-length black wig of coarse hair and a golden 18-inch tall circular headdress.

When the actor puts on the huge crown, as actors for three hundred years have done, he feels that the spirit of the god enters his body. Before he walks on stage, the actor slips a tiny seed of *chunda*, a wildflower, into each lower eyelid. Immediately the seeds irritate his eyes and make them bloodshot. The actor's red eyes glow and highlight his expressions. For hours during the night the actor uses mime, dance, and gestures, but no words, to tell the story.

Actors in Kathakali train for up to eight years and aren't expected to perfect a role until they have played it for about twenty years.

At the state-run academy in Cheruthuruthy, India, children begin training at the age of twelve. Every student is expected to master the arts of dance, mime, drumming, music, makeup, and gymnastic skills.

At 5 a.m. the students' eyeballs are lubricated with clarified butter for the eye exercises that strengthen their muscles for expressive eye movement. Their bodies are rubbed with oil and massaged so that they are flexible, and for three hours they exercise. They also learn 500 *mudras* — gestures — each with a specific meaning. As we shall see, young theater students in China and Japan train equally hard.

CHINA: THE PEKING OPERA

Peking Opera has been the most popular theatrical entertainment in China since the mid-19th century. It evolved in the late 18th century and is a mixture of spoken words, singing, music, dance, acrobatics, and gestures. Each performance consists of scenes from many plays staged without interruptions. The dramas are based on myths, folklore, legends, and romance novels. They are filled with love, the deeds of heroes, wise kings, and battles. Goodness is rewarded and evil is punished. But a play is only an outline for a performance; the actors add their own special touches to the story. Often they make changes in the script.

Centuries ago the theaters in China were called tea houses. During a performance, vendors sold melon seeds, peanuts, and tea. Attendants threw hot towels across the audience. Audience members paid for a small pot of tea, rather than a ticket, which they drank at a table on the ground floor (the equivalent of orchestra seats). They faced each other, not the stage, and came not to watch the play but to see and hear their favorite actor. Audience members still drink tea and, while the tables have disappeared, each row of seats has a shelf for the teapots.

The Staging

The stage is very simple. It is an open platform, almost square, covered by a roof that is supported by lacquered columns. Raised a few feet above the ground, it is surrounded by a wooden railing about two feet high. The stage has a carpet and two doors in the rear wall between which hangs an embroidered or painted backcloth. The door at the left is used for entrances; the door at the right is used for exits.

With such a simple stage, actors can quickly show a change of place through speech, action, or the use of a prop. This theater is controlled by very strict conventions, so everything that is done has a specific meaning. If an actor circles the stage, then the audience knows that the player is on a long journey. If he raises his knees high, then he is climbing a hill.

There are no stage settings. Instead, props are used to indicate place, to stimulate the audience's imagination so they can fill in the details in their minds. Tents, parasols, whips, paddles, and weapons are used. Swords, spears, and arrows become part of elaborate dances and parades. Tables and chairs symbolize different things according to specific arrangements that follow set rules. An incense tripod on a table indicates a palace. A table by itself might represent a hill, cloud, altar, bridge, or mountain to climb. Three chairs covered with a cloth are a bed. Two chairs back to back become a wall. One chair symbolizes a tree or the door of a prison.

If you watch a performance in the Chinese theater, you need to understand the rules. You must know, for example, that an actor who is holding a whip is riding a horse. Two yellow flags with wheels painted on them are a chariot. An oar becomes a ship. Four black banners waved by the property men symbolize a

An actor in Peking Opera. Courtesy of The Asia Society.

A Chinese dancer, Hu Hung-Yen, in Peking Opera. Courtesy of The Asia Society.

violent wind, while blue banners indicate water. If a scene requires snow, an attendant whirls a white banner and another shakes white bits of paper over the actors. You also would need to know that a red flag held before a character's face means his head was cut off, and a red sack tossed on the stage represents a severed head.

Throughout the performance assistants bring props on stage, remove them, or re-arrange them. They also help the actors with their costumes, arranging the folds of the material, for example. The assistants are not disguised, yet they are considered invisible.

The musicians sit in full view of the audience and play drums and a two-stringed violin that emits a sharp wail. When a musician isn't playing he may leave, drink tea, or read a newspaper. While music is an integral part of every show, the most important element in the Chinese theater is the actor. He must speak, sing, and move according to strict rules set by tradition. Incredible as it may seem, there are seven basic hand movements, special arm movements, more than twenty pointing gestures, twelve leg movements, even sleeve and beard movements. If an actor raises his foot, jerks his sleeve, adjusts his hat, or smoothes his beard, it has a specific meaning.

Costumes and Makeup

The sleeve on an actor's costume has a white silk cuff two feet long, and these long flowing sleeves are manipulated to convey messages, too. If a character wants to show that he is crying, he lifts the corner of his left sleeve to his eyes. Not only the sleeves but even the folds of the material in an actor's costume can convey a message.

The actor's stunning costumes made of fine materials add to the spectacle of Peking Opera. Their color and design combined with specific accessories tell the audience about each character's type, age, and social status. If you see a character in yellow, he is an emperor. A brown costume is worn by an elderly

character; black by a rough character.

Makeup is also used symbolically. There are rules for combining patterns, geometric designs, and colors to indicate specific character types and temperaments. Blue indicates a stubborn person. A loyal character has a red-painted face. Demons and outlaws appear with green paint, and gods have gold faces. Sometimes a character's face is painted in bold patterns. An actor appearing as the Monkey God would sport a triangle of crimson on his face with gold circles around his eyes and nostrils. There are many popular Chinese plays about the Monkey God who helps mankind with his superhuman abilities.

The Actors' Skills

With many battle scenes, Peking Opera often includes sword play and spectacular fights. But these scenes are staged like elaborate dances. In a duel, the actors combine acrobatics, dance, and martial arts as they whirl their swords to the clash of cymbals and pounding of drums.

For anyone who hopes to be an actor in the Chinese theater with its rigid conventions, training must begin at an early age. Most boys enter acting school between the ages of seven and twelve. During the many years of disciplined training, the boys study pantomime, hand gestures, gymnastics, voice, makeup, and movement for one to two hundred roles. Each role has its own set of movements and gestures. The boys must be able to control every gesture of the hands and the head, too.

Today males and females perform in Peking Opera, but from the late 18th century until recently actresses were forbidden. This reflected the way women in society were kept at home, away from the outside world. During this period males played the roles of women. In the 1920s the female impersonator Mei Lang Fang became famous and toured the world. He began training at age nine. In Japan female impersonators are very popular, too.

A Noh stage. Courtesy of Japan National Tourist Organization.

JAPANESE DRAMA

The Noh Plays

Noh and Kabuki are theatrical forms that developed in Japan several centuries ago from religious rituals — dances in celebration of the gods. The Noh drama is older, having begun in the 1300s and been perfected in the 1600s. If you watch a Noh production you will see it as a *shogun* — a military dictator — or emperor in the 15th century might have viewed it in a palace. These plays were written for a select audience that later included aristocrats and the wealthy. The production of these plays today is almost the same as five hundred years ago.

Most of the Noh plays staged today were written by Kanami Kiyotsugu and his son Zeami Motokiyu in the 15th century. Many are short, less than an hour long. Noh dramas are based on myths, legends, historical and religious events, novels, poetry, and diaries. There are plays about gods, emperors, warriors, ghosts, and demons. None of the dramas is easy to understand, even by Japanese audiences.

Many people watch a Noh drama and regard it as a beautiful form of art like a sculpture or a painting. The point of each play is not to develop a story or to show a conflict. In Noh drama the playwright shows some event from the past in a way that will create a mood or make people feel a certain way. A famous hero or warrior might reenact his greatest battles or a ghost might return to earth because its soul can't find peace.

The Staging

The Noh drama, a combination of dance, song, and chanted words, is performed on a stage that has remained almost unchanged since 1615. The stage, a raised platform, has a floor made of polished cypress. Under the floor are concrete cones containing sand in the bottom, so when the actors stamp their stocking feet the sound will resound. The actors beat a rhythm with their feet to suggest the emotional state of the characters they're playing.

A roof supported by four columns covers the stage, and each column has a name and a meaning. The back wall of the empty stage is a bridge that starts at the dressing room. Three potted pine trees that symbolize heaven, earth, and man line the bridgeway. White gravel on the floor divides the stage from the audience as it did centuries ago when the actors performed outdoors and white gravel separated their stage on the ground from the audience seated in a covered building.

As you sit in your chair and the curtain of five different colors is lifted by two long bamboo poles, you enter a world where every part of the performance follows a rule. Everything has a meaning including the movement of hands and feet, costumes, makeup, and props.

What Would You See On Stage?

The male actor's body is covered with white underwear and socks, then a plain silk garment, a silk kimono with beautifully embroidered designs, a wig, and a headdress. Masks, carved of wood and covered with many layers of paint, are worn by the *shite* or main actor who stars in the all-male performance. These heavy masks cover only the face and have almost no expression.

Actors respect the masks, many of which have been handed down for generations. Actors feel that they are transformed into the characters they play as soon as they put on the masks. Other actors, usually no more than six, wear colorful makeup. This includes the "child actor," a young boy about ten years old who plays the role of a child or an adult.

As in China, stage properties are simple. A bamboo frame is a boat. Hand properties are basic, too, and the most important one is the fan. It can be moving water, a rising moon, the wind blowing, or falling rain. A fan is also a tray, a knife, or a dagger.

Music is an important element in the Noh performance. A small orchestra of three or four musicians plays a flute and drums, large

and small. Their music is like the sound track of a movie to underscore the action. A chorus of three or four men sings or recites the actor's lines when he dances. The chorus and the musicians wear stiff shoulder boards and divided skirts.

The actor's movements are not lifelike but more like a series of slow and formal posturings, a dance. The actor glides his foot in its sock along the floor and points his toes high until he finishes his glide. This makes his movements slow and dignified.

In Noh there are many simple gestures that signify a complete action. One actor might tap his knee to show that he is excited. If an actor wants to show his character crying, he doesn't cry or pretend to, he raises his hand to his eyes. To indicate a mother digging in a grave where her son is buried, the actor simply spreads his arms.

Training for the Noh stage is as long and difficult as that for the Chinese theater. Actors

Artist's interpretation of a Noh mask. Illustration by Adam Broadbent.

are expected to devote at least twenty years to perfecting their art. The Noh theater is rich with tradition. It is a living museum to a time long ago when the Noh drama was first presented to the emperors and then to the warriors who ruled Japan. It is noble and quiet while Kabuki is loud, spectacular, and lively.

Kabuki

Kabuki, which means "song-dance-skill," became the most popular theatrical entertainment in Japan. It began with the dancing of O-Kuni, a female temple dancer in the 17th century. Eventually an all-female company performed, with young boys added later and finally, only men acted the Kabuki. In the 1920s it was suggested that women perform in the Kabuki again, but it was decided that women could not play the female roles as well as men could.

The male actors who play the female roles are called *onnagata* and they are very popular. Utaemon Nakamura is considered a Living National Treasure, and Tamasaburo Bando, another female impersonator, is treated like a rock star. These men are trained from early childhood to play the roles of young girls, princesses, and other women. They spend their entire lives studying female psychology and behavior and become more feminine than the women they impersonate. Even actors in their seventies can play beautiful women with skill. Until 1868 onnagata dressed in female costumes offstage, too, and were expected to act like women in their everyday life.

Romances of great heroes, characters torn between love and duty, good versus evil — these are the subjects of Kabuki plays. There are stories about heroes who are tortured by the enemy to reveal information. In one play a hero confronts an evil man who is cruel to good people. In *Kumaga Jinya* a general is ordered to deliver to his lord the head of a young man whose mother once saved his life.

Most of these dramas are episodes joined together because playwrights weren't interested in telling a complete story but, rather, in recounting a series of dramatic moments. A theatrical program made up of parts of plays lasts five hours today, but until 1850 a program lasted for twelve hours.

The Staging

The architecture of the stage for the Kabuki theater changed over time, too. Originally actors used the Noh stage. Today the Kabuki stage is as wide as the auditorium and has a proscenium arch. Flying machinery, a system of ropes and wires, is used to lift actors and let them "fly." Elevator traps in the stage floor let actors rise suddenly or quickly disappear.

A revolving stage adds to the spectacular effects. Each location in the play is suggested with scenery, usually a painted flat. Up to four scenes can be placed on different parts of the stage. The stage can be turned easily and quickly to reveal a different scene — perhaps a forest, garden, or palace. Many effects can be achieved with a revolving stage. A dull black backdrop turns into a forest of cherry blossoms. An actor can be tossed off a ship, and he can appear to swim to the other side to escape the enemy. Or an actor could wander through a forest searching for an enemy. As the set rotates, the actor walks from one scene to another.

A bridge called the *hanamichi* or "flower path" extends from the back of the auditorium to the left side of the stage. This raised runway is used for all the important entrances and exits and for dramatic scenes. The hanamichi is a garden path, a river, a mountain pass, for example. It is called the flower path because it was always lined with flowers that were given as gifts from patrons to their favorite performers.

Costumes and Makeup

The actors' costumes and makeup, combined with the elaborate scenery, add to the spectacle. One costume, consisting of layers of

Japanese Kabuki Theater showing "Flower Way." Reproduced by courtesy of the Trustees of the British Museum.

The Nakamura-za Theatre in 1859 during a Kabuki production. Courtesy of Tsubouchi Memorial Theatre Museum, Waseda University, Tokyo.

A Kabuki version of a Noh play. Courtesy of Japan National Tourist Organization.

A performer in Grand Kabuki. Courtesy of The Billy Rose Theatre Collection, The New York Public Library at Lincoln Center, Astor, Lenox, and Tilden Foundations.

The martial arts of Kabuki. Courtesy of The Asia Society.

an embroidered kimono, large brocaded over-garments or robes, long sleeves and skirt, can weigh up to fifty pounds. The actors change their costumes every time their character leaves and comes back on stage.

One of the most sensational moments in a Kabuki play is when an actor changes his character and his clothes onstage. The actor's outer garments are lightly sewn together so when the attendant breaks some of the threads, the first costume falls to the floor and the next costume is revealed. In the play *Ogiya Kumagai*, the character Atsumori is disguised as a girl, but suddenly the over-garment falls and Atsumori reveals his true identity as he stands in full armor.

The actor's makeup creates a beautiful and colorful picture and tells a lot about the character he plays. Ladies and romantic young men wear white makeup while married women have stained teeth. A character with superhuman power has red lines running over his face that look like swollen blood vessels.

The Actor

The most important aspect of the Kabuki is the actor, who recites his lines in a singsong, chanting way and moves in bare feet or light-colored socks like a dancer. The acting is not realistic. The actors don't try to act naturally the way real people do. Instead they pose and use gestures to convey a message. At dramatic moments an actor will freeze like a statue with his eyes wide open, sometimes crossing them or looking fierce.

Like other actors in Eastern theaters, performers in the Kabuki begin their long and intensive studies when they are six or seven years old. The students study acting, dancing, and singing as well as how to play the *samisen*, a stringed instrument, how to conduct a tea ceremony, Japanese flower arranging, and calligraphy. Since there are many roles for children in Kabuki plays, students get to perform onstage at an early age. Most actors, however, are not considered mature players

until they are in their mid-forties.

A Kabuki performance is full of energy, noise, motion, and spectacle. A bell rings, calling people to their seats and then an attendant, dressed in black, claps two square hardwood sticks. The rhythm he beats is different for each play and serves to set the mood. The excitement builds as the curtain of black, brown, and green is pushed to the right of the brightly lit stage.

The musicians accompany the action with flutes, drums, bells, gongs, cymbals, and stringed instruments. A chorus sings and explains the action. Heroes, villains, and noblemen pose or strut across the stage. Large numbers of characters crowd the stage for battle scenes. Dances take over at any moment, scenes change swiftly, a costume falls to the floor to reveal another, colors swirl, dozens of attendants move properties and help the actors with their costumes. The performance is stunning and exciting.

Since the early days of Kabuki, the set rules and acting styles have been passed down within a small number of families, from father to son. Most stars today are descendants of earlier actors, and there are some families whose line of actors goes back to the 17th century. A Kabuki family that doesn't have an heir can adopt a pupil to keep the family acting tradition going. If an actor is the only son in a famous acting family, he is not allowed to leave the profession, even if he is not a good actor.

Today there are several large theaters in Japan that specialize in presenting Kabuki. They receive financial support from the government. Kabuki companies tour all over the world including the United States.

EASTERN THEATER TOUCHES THE WESTERN WORLD

Acting companies from Japan and China first toured the Western world in the 19th century. The West translated some of the Oriental plays and imitated Eastern costumes. They borrowed some of the staging ideas like revolving stages and a runway through the audience. Directors and playwrights experimented with using scenery, costumes, and gestures in addition to words to convey meaning, after seeing Eastern dramas. As recently as 1976 composer Stephen Sondheim and director Harold Prince used elements of Kabuki in the American musical *Pacific Overtures*.

As you have traveled through time from the beginnings of the theater toward the present, you've met many dedicated people, adults and children, some of whom have struggled and sacrificed much to participate in the theater. If you continue the journey through the 18th, 19th, and 20th centuries, you will find determined, persevering, and talented theater people, too.

Japanese Kabuki dancer Sachiyo Ito. Courtesy of The Asia Society.

GLOSSARY

Amphitheater — In ancient Rome, a large round or oval outdoor theater with tiers of raised seats surrounding an open central arena. It was originally used for gladiatorial contests. The Colosseum is the most famous example of an amphitheater.

Apron — Large open platform that extends in front of the proscenium arch and into the auditorium. Actors and actresses performed here, especially during the English Restoration.

Autos sacramentales — Spanish term for a religious play. Usually associated with the celebration of Corpus Christi, these plays combine the features of medieval cycle plays and morality plays. They have human, supernatural, and allegorical characters and are based on Biblical stories and sacred events.

Border — A piece of scenery made of cloth or wood that is placed horizontally across the top of the set. It is usually used to mask lighting or other technical devices.

Capa y espada — Literally, "cloak and sword," a type of drama popular in Spain during the 16th and 17th centuries. They are stories of love, romance, adventure, intrigue, and honor centering on the everyday lives of aristocratic and middle class gentlemen. The drama derives its name from the clothing gentlemen wore in these plays, which included a circular cape and a sword.

Carros — In Spain, large flat or two-story wagons which carried scenery and players and served as stages. They moved through the streets to several stopping places where a play was enacted.

Choregus, *pl.* **choregoi** — In Greek theater, a rich and important citizen who paid the playwright's production costs including costumes, props, musicians, and the training of the chorus.

City Dionysia — A week-long Athenian spring festival in honor of the god Dionysus. It became an annual play-producing festival in the fifth century B.C. where tragedies, comedies, and satyr plays were presented by three playwrights in the form of a contest.

Closet drama — A play written to be read, not staged. The plays of the Roman dramatist Seneca are closet dramas.

Comédias — In Spain these are secular or non-religious plays. They include any full-length play, comedy or tragedy. Comédias are based on folklore, legends, history, mythology, and everyday life.

Comedy of manners — A type of drama that pictures the complicated intrigues of the rich and elegant men and women of the upper classes and is told with witty dialogue. It is often associated with the English Restoration and the plays of William Wycherley and William Congreve.

Commedia dell'arte — Literally "comedy of professional artists." It was the popular theater of the Italian Renaissance and the first theater with professional actors in organized companies. Actors played character types, wore masks, and improvised most of the play on simple platforms.

Corpus Christi play — A medieval religious play associated with the Feast of Corpus Christi. Produced most often in England and Spain.

Corrales — In Spain, the courtyards closed in by neighboring buildings and in which plays were staged. The corrales were controlled by religious orders of the Catholic Church.

Cycle play — One-act plays grouped together and presented in order. In medieval England, it was a series of mystery plays presenting Bible history from the Creation of the Universe to the Day of Judgment.

Deus ex machina—Literally, "god from the machine." In Greek drama, a god was often lowered in a crane at the end of the play to resolve all conflicts.

Dionysus—The Greek god of wine and fertility. Also known as the Greek god of drama.

Dithyramb—In ancient Greece, a hymn or poem to honor Dionysus, chanted and danced to by a chorus of fifty men dressed in goatskins.

Downstage—The area of the stage closest to the audience; the front of the stage. The term originated when the stage was raked or tilted so that the front part was lower than or down from the back part of the stage.

Dramatist—The individual who writes a play.

Ekkyklema—In Greek theater, a platform or couch on wheels. It was used to roll out bodies of characters killed offstage.

Farce—Type of comedy with exaggerated characters and ridiculous situations, with much horseplay and physical humor.

Flat—Light wooden frame covered with canvas or fabric, it is often painted to resemble part of a wall. Can be arranged on stage as part of the scenery.

Groundlings—In Shakespearean theater, the people who stood in the open courtyard of the theater to watch the play. So called because they had their feet on the ground.

Guild (*Greek*) — Professional organizations composed of all the individuals needed to produce a play: playwrights, actors, chorus members, musicians, and costumers.

Guild (*Middle Ages*) — An association of craftsmen or merchants. Guild members often produced and financed a play annually as their contribution to a religious festival.

Hanamichi—Also known as the "flower path." In Kabuki theater this is the bridge or raised runway that extends from the back of the auditorium to the left side of the stage. It is used by actors for entrances and exits.

Heroic drama—Tragedies in which the hero and heroine agonize over fulfilling their love for each other versus meeting the demands of honor and duty to their country or family.

Improvisation—Situation in which the performers make up the dialogue and the action on the spur of the moment during a performance. Often associated with the actors of the commedia dell'arte.

Interlude—In medieval England this was a short play with a small cast and little scenery, presented at a court banquet. It usually had a moral and dealt with a religious or political idea.

Intermezzo, *pl.* **intermezzi**—A comic performance with a mythological or Biblical theme presented between the acts of a play during the Italian Renaissance.

Jig—In Shakespearean theater, a short music and dance piece that ended most plays.

Kathakali—A popular stylized dance–drama in Kerala, located on the southwest tip of India. Actors wear elaborate, colorful costumes and use mime, dance, and gestures to tell a story.

Lazzi—In commedia dell'arte these were jokes—stunts, gestures, witty comments, and speeches—that had little to do with the play but added humor.

Liturgical drama—Also called "church drama." These were plays based on stories from the Bible, acted by priests and choirboys as part of the church services. They were performed indoors and chanted in Latin.

Ludi Romani—In Roman theater, a religious festival in honor of the god Jupiter. Plays and other entertainment including rope dancing and circus races were offered to please the god.

Machine play—A type of 17th century French play that featured mechanical wonders including flying characters and dazzling scene changes.

Mansion—In medieval drama, a miniature room with no wall in front that housed simple props and furniture. It was used as an acting area.

Masque—An entertainment that relies on a

combination of dance music, elegant scenery, and costumes. Often presented as a court entertainment that glorified the ruler before whom it was presented.

Mechane — In ancient Greek theater, a crane used to show characters in flight or suspended above earth. See **Deus ex machina**.

Mime — In Roman theater, a short play with a simple story-line often about a situation from everyday life. Unlike the modern mime who is silent, the Roman mime spoke.

Miracle play — Medieval play that dramatizes the lives of saints, martyrs, the Virgin Mary, and other religious stories not found in the Bible.

Morality play — Medieval drama in which the characters represent abstractions like Truth or Beauty. They sought to teach the audience a moral lesson while entertaining them. *Everyman* is the most famous morality play.

Mosqueteros — In 16th and 17th century Spain, these were the spectators who stood in the patio, or open space, of the outdoor theaters. The success or failure of a play often depended on their reaction to it.

Mudras — Gestures used by the performer in the Indian dance–drama Kathakali. There are 500 mudras, each with a specific meaning.

Mummer's play — A medieval English entertainment in which amateur actors entered a king's or nobleman's banquet hall disguised in masks and costumes. The merriment ended in a dance.

Mystery play — A medieval play based on a story from the Old or New Testament. It was presented in the native language and staged outside the church.

Neoclassical drama — Play based on an interpretation of Greek and Roman dramatic principles. The best examples are from 17th century France, particularly the tragedies of Jean Racine.

Noh — The short classical dance–drama of Japan. It originated in the 13th century and is a combination of dance, song, and chanted words. Noh is based on myths and legends and

is designed to create a mood rather than tell a complete story.

Oberammergau — Bavarian town in the Alps of West Germany. It is the setting for *The Passion Play*, which is produced every ten years. It began in 1634 when the townspeople vowed to perform the passion play if a plague was lifted from their community.

Onnagata — In Japanese Kabuki, the male actors who play female roles. They are very popular performers who can play these roles until they are quite old.

Opera — Theatrical form developed by the Italians in the 1590s in which the story is told through words sung to a musical accompaniment. Opera relies on music, spectacular sets, costumes, and mechanical devices.

Orchestra — In Greek theater, the flat circular area where the chorus and actors performed. In Roman theater, the semi-circular ground-level acting area. In a modern theater, the main ground-level section of the audience.

Pageant play — One of the terms used for a medieval play.

Pageant wagon — In medieval England, the wagon or cart was a high and large mansion on wheels. It held simple pieces of furniture and properties to suggest a scene. It was pulled from place to place where it was used as an acting space or as a background for the performance.

Pantomime — In ancient Rome, a dramatic form that starred one masked dancer who silently told a story through movement and gesture. The performer was accompanied by music and a chorus who sang the story-line, often on the theme of love.

Paradoi — In ancient Greece, the passageways or side entrances between the skene, the background, and the theatron or area where the audience sat. Paradoi were used primarily for the entrances and exits of the chorus.

Paraskenia — In ancient Greek theater, the rectangular rooms projecting in front of the skene on both sides. They served as the dressing rooms for the actors and the chorus.

Passion play — A medieval drama that treats the Crucifixion of Jesus Christ and his Resurrection.

Pastoral — A short play, usually a love story about shepherds and nymphs, which takes place in a perfect countryside where life is quiet, happy, and simple. Aristocratic women enjoyed acting in pastorals, especially during the Italian Renaissance.

Periaktoi — In ancient Greek theater during the Hellenistic period, these were tall, triangular prisms set at either side of the skene. Scenes were painted or hung on each side. The periaktoi revolved to suggest a change of location.

Pinakes — In ancient Greek theater, these were painted canvases in wooden frames set in front of the skene to suggest the location of the play. They were introduced by the playwright Aeschylus.

Platea — The word means "place." In medieval theater this was the wide, empty central area in a cathedral or church that was used as an acting space.

Playlet — A short play in a cycle during the Middle Ages. An example is "The Building of the Ark."

Playwright — An individual who writes a play. In ancient Greece, the playwright also directed the play, planned the dances, trained the dancers, wrote the music, and often played the leading role.

Plot — The story of a play or the sequence of scenes in a play. In Shakespearean theater this also referred to a sheet of paper hanging from a nail on the backstage wall, listing the sequence of scenes in the play, the names of the actors needed in each scene, and the actors' entrances and exits.

Properties — Also referred to as "props." Items used in the play other than costumes, furniture, and scenery. These objects include flowers, fans, swords, and books, for example.

Proscenium arch — The large picture frame or wall that divides the acting area or stage from the audience.

Pundonor — Spanish term meaning "code of honor." The code stated that a man must defend his family name and honor if they were attacked. This was a theme used in many Spanish comédias.

Raked — A stage floor that is tilted or angled. Beginning in the Italian Renaissance, the stage floor was sloped or tilted up at a sharp angle to the back. The rear of the stage floor was higher than the front of the floor.

Rasas — The mood or "flavor" around which each play in classical Indian drama was developed. There are nine rasas including love, sorrow, anger, horror, and wonder.

Role — A performer's part in a play.

Round — In medieval theater this was the flat, round, open area surrounded by an earth embankment that was dug out of an open field. Raised scaffolds on the inside of the round seated spectators who watched the medieval plays that were staged there.

Satyr play — In ancient Greek theater, a short comedy that poked fun at the theme or story presented in the tragedies that preceded it. The satyr play developed from the dithyramb.

Scaenae frons — In ancient Roman theater, the elaborate stage wall used as the background for the action. It was two to three stories high and decorated with columns and statues. It represented the front of a building in tragedies and a series of houses in comedies.

Scenario — A scene by scene outline or basic plot of the action of a commedia dell'arte play.

Set — The surroundings or scenery in which a play takes place.

Set piece — A piece of stage scenery cut out of a flat. It might represent a house or a fountain, for example. The term also refers to a three-dimensional piece of scenery. An example is the Hell Mouth in medieval drama.

Shite — The main actor who stars in the all-male performance of Noh drama in Japan.

Sides — In Shakespearean theater, the written copy of an actor's lines and entrance cues. It was written on a scroll which the actor unrolled during rehearsals.

Skene — In ancient Greek theater, the building behind the playing area. At various times used as a storage room, changing room, and background for the action. It evolved from a small room to a large structure. From it we get our word "scene."

Slapstick — In commedia dell'arte, the wooden bat made of two hinged sticks that clap loudly together when the bat is used to hit someone.

Spectacle — In general, any entertainment that relies on dazzling effects, especially visual and technical wonders. In ancient Roman theater, it refers to entertainments offering bloodshed and violence, such as gladiatorial combats and sea battles.

Stock character — A basic character type who always speaks the same and reacts to a situation in a certain way. Often wears a standard costume and mask, especially in Roman comedy and in the commedia dell'arte.

Subplot — The secondary plot or story-line in a play. Often relates to or underscores the main plot.

Theatron — A Greek word meaning "seeing place" and from which we derive the word "theater." In the ancient Greek theater it was the place where the audience sat. It consisted of tiers of seats surrounding a playing space in a horseshoe all the way up the hillside.

Thespian — A Greek word meaning "dramatic" or "actor." It is derived from Thespis, the earliest known playwright and actor. He is said to have won the first dramatic competition.

Tiring house — In Shakespearean theater, the term for the players' dressing rooms. It was located behind the back wall of the stage.

Tragicomedy — Plays that mix elements of comedy and tragedy. They are serious plays but they include comic touches and end happily. Francis Beaumont and John Fletcher were noted for writing tragicomedies in 17th century England.

Trope — Chanted words that were put to music and incorporated into the Catholic Church service during the 10th century.

Troupe — A company of actors.

Upstage — The rear of the stage. The name is derived from a time beginning in the Italian Renaissance when the stage floor was tilted at an angle so that the rear of the stage was up or higher than the front of the stage.

Vomitorium, *pl.* **vomitoria** — In ancient Roman theater, the doors in each section of each level of the auditorium. So named because they spit out or "vomit" spectators out of the seating areas.

Zanni — A comic servant in a commedia dell'arte play. These acrobats, dancers, funmakers kept the plays lively with their antics, tricks, and exaggerated expressions.

SUGGESTED READING

Brockett, Oscar G. *The Essential Theatre,* Fourth Edition. New York: Rinehart and Winston, Inc., 1988.

Chute, Marchette. *An Introduction to Shakespeare.* New York: E. P. Dutton and Co., Inc., 1951.

Geisinger, Marion. *Plays, Players and Playwrights.* New York: Hart Publishing, 1971.

Hartnoll, Phyllis. *The Concise History of Theatre.* New York: N. Abrams, n.d.

Harwood, Ronald. *All the World's a Stage.* Boston: Little, Brown and Co., 1984.

Hodges, C. Walter. *Shakespeare's Theatre.* New York: Coward–McCann, Inc., 1964.

Mitchley, Jack and Peter Spaulding. *Five Thousand Years of the Theatre.* London: Batsford Academic and Educational Ltd., 1982.

Papp, Joseph and Elizabeth Kirkland. *Shakespeare Alive!.* New York: Bantam Books, 1988.

Smiley, Sam. *Theatre: The Human Art.* New York: Harper & Row, 1987.

INDEX

A

Actors, 12, 14, 19, 27, 33, 34, 35,
    81–2, 95, 97, 105, 107, 117
    female, 117
    first, 14
    French, 105, 107
    Greek, 12, 19, 27
        photo, 12
    in Elizabethan theater, 81–2
    Roman, 33, 34, 35
        illustration, 34
        photo, 34
    Spanish, 95, 97
Aeschylus, 15, 19, 22, 24
Affected Ladies, The, 104
Alchemist, The, 86
Alexander the Great, 27
Alexandre, 103
All for Love, 113
Alleyn, Edward, 82
    portrait, photo, 82
American Repertory Theater, 93
American Shakespeare Theater,
    76
Andreini, Isabella, 67
Andromaque, 103
Anne, 119
Antolin, Antonia Lopez, 97
Antony and Cleopatra, 80, 86,
    113
Apron, 115
Architettura, 56
Aristophanes, 19, 25
Aristotle, 22, 101
Armani, Vincenza, 67
Asian theater, 121–33
Autos sacramentales, 89, 90
    illustration, 90

B

Barry, Elizabeth, 117
Beaumont, Francis, 86

Behn, Aphra, 115
Bellerose, 107
Betterton, Thomas, 117
Blackfriars, 86
Borders, 59
Bracegirdle, Anne, 117
Burbage, James, 73, 75
Burbage, Richard, 81, 82, 84

C

Cabanas, Antonio, 97
Caldéron, Pedro, 89, 91, 92, 93
    portrait, photo, 92
Capa y espada plays, 91
Capello, Bianca, 53
Carros, 89
Catholic Church, conflict with
    theater, 39
Charles I, 86
Charles II, 111, 113, 115, 117, 119
Chinoy, Helen Krich, 9
Chock, Denny, 117
Choregus, 12
Christine of Lorraine, 53
Church of St.-Denis, France,
    illustration, 40
Cicero, 31
Cinna, 103
Circus Maximus, 29, 36, 37
City Dionysia, 11, 12–3, 22
Closet dramas, 35
Clouds, The, 19, 25
Clytemnestra, 37
Collier, Jeremy, 119
Colosseum, 36, 37
    photo, 36
Comédias, 90–1
Comédie–Française, 108, 109
    photo, 108
Comedy, Greek, 25
Comedy of Errors, The, 31, 80

Comedy of manners, 113, 115
    characters, 113, 115
    plots, 113
Commedia dell'arte, 61, 63–7,
    68, 69
    illustrations, 64, 66
    photos, 68, 69
    stock characters, 64–7
    troupes, 67
Condell, Henry, 77
Confrèrie de la Passion, 99
Congreve, William, 113
Conquest of Granada, The, 113
Corneille, Pierre, 101, 102, 103
    portrait, photo, 102
Cornish Mystery Cycle, 43
    photo, 44
Corpus Christi plays, 42
Corral de Comédias de Ciudad
    Real, photo, 96
Corral de la Cruz, 94
Corral del Principe, 94
Corrale theater, illustration, 93
Corrales, 93–4
Country Wife, The, 113
Curmudgeon, The, 25
Curtain, The, 76
Cycle plays, 42, 43, 45, 48–9, 50
    actors, 50
    sets, 43
    staging, 48–9

D

Davenant, William, 111, 115
De Soto, Bernardo, 94
Death of Pompey, The, 103
Dell'Arte Players, 68
Demetrius, 33
Deus ex machina, 19
Dionysus, 11
Dithyramb, 11
Drury Lane, 115

Dryden, John, 113
Duchess of Malfi, The, 86
Duke's Company, 115

E
Edward II, 76
Ekkyklema, 19, 22
Elizabeth I, 73, 74, 75, 76, 86
    illustration, 74
Elizabethan theater, 81–2, 83–6
    actors, 81–2
    audience, 83
    staging, 83–6
English plays, first, 73
English Restoration theater,
    111–9
    actors, 117–8
    actresses, 117
    comedy of manners, 113, 115
    illustration, 114
    performance, 119
    playhouses, 115
    playwrights, 115
    staging, 115–6
English theater, 71–88, 115
    after Elizabeth, 86, 88
    playwrights, 76, 115
    Puritan reaction, 86, 88
Epidaurus, *see* Theater at
    Epidaurus
Equus, 22
Etherege, George, 113
Eucharis, 35
Euripides, 22, 24
    statue of, photo, 24
Everyman, 51

F
Farces, 50
Farquhar, George, 113
Ferdinando I, 53
Field, Nathaniel, 73
Fiesta de los Carros, 89
First Folio, 77
Flats, 56
Fletcher, John, 86
Fortune, The, 76
Francesco I, 53
French neoclassical theater,
    99–109
    actors, 105, 107
    performance, illustration,
        100

French neoclassical theater,
    continued
    staging, 108–9
*Funny Thing Happened on the
    Way to the Forum, A*, 31
Furies, The, 19

G
Garrigo, Cristobal, 97
Gelosi, 67
Globe, The, 75, 76, 80–1, 84,
    85, 86, 88
    model, photograph, 85
    illustration, 75
Gorboduc, 73
Greek theater, 11–28, 31
    actors, 19, 20, 26, 27
        photo, 20, 26
    chorus, 18
    comedy, 25
    costumes, 18–9
    design, 27
    Hellenistic age, 25, 27
    masks, 18–9, 27
        photo, 18
    New Comedy, 25, 27, 31
    Old Comedy, 25, 27
    playing area, 15, 17–8
    playwrights, 22, 24
    staging, 19
Greek tragedy, 22, 24
Groundlings, 83
Guilds, 27, 42, 50
Gwyn, Eleanor (Nell), 116, 117
    portrait, photo, 116

H
Hamlet, 77
Hanamichi, 128
Hartley, Elizabeth, illustration,
    103
Hell Mouth, 45, 46
    illustration, 45
Heminges, John, 76
Henri IV, 67
Henry IV, 80
Henry VI, 80
Henry VIII, 84
Heroic dramas, 113
Hôtel de Bourgogne, 108, 109
Horace, 103
House of Fire, 37

I
Imaginary Invalid, The,
    illustration, 106
Improvisation, 64
Indian theater, 121–3
    Kathakali, 122, 123
    playwriting, 121, 123
Inn yards, 71–3
    illustration, 72
Interludes, 50
Intermezzi, 55
Italian Renaissance, 53–69
    commedia dell'arte, 61, 63–7
    scenery, 56–9, 60
        illustration, 60
    theaters, 55
    types of drama, 55

J
James I, 86
Japanese drama, 126–32
    Kabuki, 128–32
    Noh plays, 126–8
Jew of Malta, The, 76
Jones, Inigo, 86
Jonson, Ben, 80, 86, 88
Justinian, 37

K
Kabuki, 128–32
    actors, 132
    costumes and makeup, 128,
        132
    illustrations, 129, 130
    photos, 131
    staging, 128
Kalidasa, 121
Kanami Kiyotsugu, 126
Kathakali, 122, 123
    photos, 122
Killigrew, Thomas, 111, 115
King John, 77
King Lear, 77, 79, 80
    photo, 79
King's Men, 77, 115
King's Players, 105
King's Servants, 115
Kumaga Jinya, 128
Kyd, Thomas, 76
Kynaston, Edward, 84

L
Jast Judgment, 49
Lazzi, 65
Le Cid, 101, 102
    illustration, 102
Life Is a Dream, 93
Little Clay Cart, The, 121
Liturgical drama, 39, 41
Livius Andronicus, 29
Lord Admiral's Men, 82
Lord Chamberlain's Men, 80, 82
Louis XIII, 99
Louis XIV, 99, 104, 109
Love for Love, 112, 113
    photo, 112
Ludi Romani, 29
Lyly, John, 76

M
Macbeth, 77
Maison de Molière, 109
Man of Mode, The, 113
Mansion, 41, 43
Marcus Aurelius, 36
Marlowe, Christopher, 76, 82, 88
Mary, 119
Masks, 18–9, 25, 27, 33, 34, 45
    devil, photo, 45
    Greek, 18–9, 27
        illustration, 19
    illustration, 25
    Roman, 33, 34
        illustration, 25
    Roman, 33, 34
        photo, 34
Masques, 86
Mazarin, Jules, 99
Mechane, 19
Medea, 24
Medieval theater, 39–52
    cycle plays, 43, 45
    liturgical drama, 39, 41
    morality plays, 51
    outdoor plays, 42
    plays produced, 42–3
    production of, 42
    secular drama, 50–1
    special effects, 46–8
Meggs, Mary, 117
Mei Lang Fang, 125
Menander, 25, 30

Methia, Richard, 9
Midsummer Night's Dream, A, 77
Mime, 35
Minstrels, 39
Miracle plays, 42
Miser, The, 104
Molière, 67, 103–5, 109
    as Sganarelle, illustration, 105
    portrait, photo, 105
Morality plays, 51
Mosqueteros. 94
Mudras, 123
Mummer's plays, 50
Mystery plays, 42

N
Neoclassical dramas, 55
Nero, 35
New York Shakespeare Festival, 76
Noh plays, 126–8
    actors, 127–8
    costumes and makeup, 127
    masks, 127
        illustration, 127
    staging, 126–7
Norton, Thomas, 73
Nursery, 119

O
Oberammergau, 51–2
    photo, 51
Oedipus Rex, 18, 22, 23, 24
    photo, 23
Ogiya Kumagai, 132
O–Kuni, 128
Onnagata, 128
Opera, 55
Orange girls, 117
Orchestra, 17, 27, 31
Oresteia, The, 22
Origins of theater, 11
Osiris Passion Play, 11
Othello, 77

P
Pacific Overtures, 133
Pageant plays, 42
Pageant wagon, 49–50
Pantomime, 35

Paradoi, 18
Paraskenia, 17
Parterre, 108
Passion Play, The, 51
Passion plays, 42, 46
    illustration, 46
Pastorals, 55
Pavy, Saloman, 73
Peking Opera, 123–5
    actors, 125
    costumes and makeup, 125
    photos, 124
    staging, 124–5
Periaktoi, 27
Perspective, 56
Phantom Lady, The, 91, 93
Phèdre, 103
Philip II, 94
Philippe, 104
Philips, Katherine, 115
Phokion, 12
Pinakes, 22
Platea, 41
Plautus, 30, 31, 55, 77
Playhouses, permanent, 73, 75
Playlet, 50
Playwrights, 11–2, 22, 24, 76, 115
    English, 76
    first female, 115
    Greek, 11–2, 22, 24
Playwrights' contest, 11–2
Plot, 82
Poetics, The, 22
Polyeucte, 103
Pompey, 31
Poquelin, Jean Baptiste, *see* Molière
Prince, Harold, 133
Prince of Orange's Players, The, 99, 105
Protagoras, 53
Pundonor, 91
Puritans, 71, 111

Q
Quem Queritis, 39, 41
Quintus Roscius Gallus, *see* Roscius

R

Racine, Jean, 103
Raked stage, 56
Ralph Roister Doister, 73
Rasas, 121
Red Bull, The, 76
Renaissance, *see* Italian
    Renaissance
Restoration, *see* English
    Restoration
Richard III, 79, 80
    photo, 79
Richelieu, 99, 101
Road Company, The, 68
Roman theater, 29–37
    actors, 33, 34, 35
        illustration, 34
        photo, 34
    as spectacle, 36–7
    Christian opposition to, 37
    comedies, 30–1
    festivals, 29, 30
        illustration, 30
    masks, 33
        photo, 32
    staging, 29–30, 31, 33
    story line, 35
    tragedy, 35
Romeo and Juliet, 76, 77, 85, 111
Roscius, 33
Rose, The, 76, 87, 88
    excavation, 88
    photos, 87
Roules, Pierre, 104
Rounds, 43
Royal Shakespeare Theatre, 76
Rueda, Lope de, 93

S

Sachiyo Ito, photo, 133
Sackville, Thomas, 73
Satyr plays, 11–2
Satyrs, 11
Scaenae frons, 31
Second Shepherd's Play, The, 48
Seneca, 35, 55

Serlio, Sebastiano, 56–9
    scenery, illustrations, 57, 58
Sganarelle, 104
Shakespeare, William, 31, 67,
    76–7, 80–1, 84, 86, 88, 101,
    104, 111, 113
    portrait, photo, 77
Shakespearean theater, 71–88
Shakuntala, 121
*Short View of the Immorality
    and Profaneness of the
    English Stage, A*, 119
Skene, 17, 27
Socrates, 25
Solon, 14
Sondheim, Stephen, 133
Sophocles, 15, 22, 24
Spanish theater, 89–97
    actors, 95, 97
    capa y espada plays, 91
    Church opposition to, 97
    comédias, 90–1
    influences, 89
    religious plays, 89–90
    staging, 93–5
Spanish Tragedy, The, 76
Stratford, Ontario Festival
    Theatre, 76
Stratocles, 33
Sulla, 33
Surgeon of His Honor, The, 91
Swan, The, 76, 85
    illustration, 85

T

Tamasaburo Bando, 128
Tamburlaine the Great, 76
Taming of the Shrew, The, 77, 78
    photo, 78
Tartuffe, 104
Teatro Farnese, 54, 55
    photos, 54
Terence, 30–1, 55
Theater at Epidaurus, 13, 17,
    18, 20, 21
    photos, 13, 17, 20, 21

Theater of Dionysus, photo, 16
Theatre, The, 75, 80
Théâtre du Marais, 99, 108, 109
Théâtre Illustre, 104
Théâtre Italien, 67
Théâtre–Français, 109
Theatre Royal, 115
Theatron, 17
Theodora, 37
Thespian, 14
Thespis, 14
Tiring House, 83
Tooley, Nicholas, 84
*Tragical History of Doctor
    Faustus, The*, 76
Tragicomedies, 86
Trojan Women, The, 24
Tropes, 39, 41
Troupe, 52
Two Gentlemen of Verona, The,
    76, 78
    photo, 78

U

Udall, Nicholas, 73
Uffizi Theatre, 55
Unities, 101
"University-Wits," 76
Utaemon Nakamura, 128

V

Vega, Lope de, 91
Vitruvius, 55
Volpone, 86
Vomitoria, 33

W

Way of the World, The, 113
Webster, John, 86
West Side Story, 76
William, 119
Wycherley, William, 113

Z

Zanni, 65
Zeami Motokiyu, 126